IF MY
People

Prayers for Healing, Hope, & Restoration

ANTHOLOGY COMPILED BY
CYNTHIA KNIGHT

IF MY PEOPLE: PRAYERS FOR HEALING, HOPE, AND RESTORATION

Copyright © 2021 compiled by CYNTHIA KNIGHT

All rights reserved. No part of this book may be reproduced or transmitted in any form or by any means without written permission from the author.

ISBN 978-0-9852542-7-8

Printed in the United States of America

Published in USA by Onyx Gavel Publishing

A subsidiary of Mosaic Consortium Group, LLC.

www.onyxgavel.com

publish@onyxgavel.com

Contents

HEALING AND RESTORATION 5
HOPE 21
PRAISE AND THANKS 29
WORSHIP AND ADORATION 39
MORNING DEVOTIONALS 45
GOD HELP ME, SAVE ME 53
GRIEF, LOSS, AND BROKEN HEARTED 67
DELIVERANCE 85
SPIRITUAL WARFARE 93
GLOBAL PRAYERS 105
PETITION PRAYERS 123
CONTRIBUTING AUTHORS 143
REFERENCES 173

DEDICATION

This book is dedicated to all my intercessors and prayer warriors who have covered me all my life. My Godparents Pastor Ronald and First Lady Dorothy Statham, and my first prayer teacher, my Mother Cornelia L. King. You taught me to keep God first and encouraged me to keep going every day. I love you.

Introduction

I'm so grateful and honored to be able to introduce this work to you. However, I must admit I was not ready or prepared when God brought the vision of this book to me, in the shower, of all places. I was actually working on another project. If I'm honest, I struggled to write the other book, which I strongly felt that God was leading me to write, when God brought this book to me. I questioned if I had heard God correctly the first time or misheard him *this* time. God had already given me the answer weeks prior, but I didn't realize it.

I belong to a writing community called Flourish Writers. During one particular session, we were sharing our book premises and receiving feedback. A fellow Flourish writer reluctantly shared her book premise because she had struggled with it and thought she was missing the mark. However, when she shared the idea for her book, I and many others fell in love with her book project idea and were excited to hear more about it at future meetings. When we convened again, she reported that God had taken her in a different direction, and she presented another premise, which, I must admit, left me baffled. I thought to myself was that really God or had she talked herself out of a spectacular book just because of insecurity and uncertainty.

The answer in both cases, mine and hers, is God is multi-faceted and multi-dimensional. He operates inside and outside of time. The reality is we must be willing to change course when God says change course, without hesitation. The Israelites 40 years of wandering in the desert ended with one change of course, even though the journey was required. It is similar to how we use a comma in punctuation for a brief pause in a sentence. God can put a comma in our lives and in time, but it's just a brief pause… delayed is not denial. So, I consider this book a God comma, and everything else is God's will, in His time.

Recently, I was talking and catching up with my Godfather. At the time of our conversation, life, as for so many, was hitting both of us hard. He was recovering from heart surgery and battling other health issues when his wife, my Godmother, received a bad news report from the doctor, which required that she also have surgery. Despite this precarious situation, my Godfather declared, "whenever you pray do you know the one thing you should always pray?

"No," I replied. My Godfather said you should pray, "God, please condition me for your will, condition me to accept whatever your will is for my life." I just gasped. It was an overwhelming revelation. What you want, what you plan, how you think or imagined your life to be just may not be the will of God for you. If you are conditioned for God's will, you will not be disappointed if he chooses not to fulfill your plan. Not to mention, you may need extra strength and faith to endure whatever God's Plan or Will is for your life. It may be overwhelming. To which my Godfather added, imagine a plate full of food, like a Thanksgiving plate. You see all the different items on the plate, and it is brimming over. "How do you eat a plate full of food?" The answer, one forkful at a time. He ended our conversation with God said, my grace is sufficient. He won't put more on us than we can bear. However, we must endure, one forkful at a time.

That was such a revelatory word for me, and I offer it to you in this season, whatever you may be going through. Everyone's plate is full in this turbulent season. I know firsthand because I'm not sure I would be writing again in this particular season of my life if it had been left up to me. Since the pandemic began, the challenges that I have endured with my health, family, and job were enough for me to deal with and quickly put writing on the back burner, but this was the exact time God chose to perform a Lazarus type resurrection on my writing career. Thank God it was not left up to me. He introduced me to a fantastic writing group and entrusted me with four books to birth, this being the second one, all during a pandemic and substantial health issues. God's Grace is sufficient. I felt like Sarah when she laughed, but we all know God had the last laugh.

This brings us to today. This book is a God-orchestrated work to assist those struggling to pray or feeling the need to reach out to God, maybe for the first time.

God blessed me with twenty-five phenomenal men and women of God who did not hesitate to come on board at my first request. I did not have to convince anyone, twist any arms, and I did not have to follow up with one person. God even performed a miracle by providing a contributing author that I had never met.

I often use the Bible App for my prayer and meditation time, and I was particularly moved by a devotion I read in a bible plan called *Everything I Need* within the app. Then I felt God leading me to reach out to the author of this bible plan, but I had to find her first. It only took a day. I reached out on LinkedIn of all places, and she too agreed to participate in this project within one day *without knowing me at all*. That's nothing but God, people.

When God tells you to do something, no matter how crazy it sounds to you, just know He will provide for His will to come to pass. It just requires our obedience and not leaning to our understanding of things.

So my unyielding gratitude goes out to all my contributing authors who labored, prayed, and fasted with me to bring this work of prayers to you. I honor and thank each of them:

*Elder Darryl D. Brookins * Minister A. Lynae Brooks * Mya Jackson Brown * Minister Angelique M. Bullock * LaShaviar S. Burns * Evangelist Teraleen R. Campbell * Cassandra Epps * Pastor P.M. Finley * Terralyn Frazier * Toni G. Guy * Evangelist Elaine Harmon * Minister Melissa Powell-Harrell * Minister Mishawn A. Jones * Cynthia Knight * Minister Michelle Lee Holly Magnuson * Renee Myers * Nicki Nichols * Elder Elect Sonja Owens * Brian Pinson * Elder Alicia A. Richardson * Amanda B. Sumiel * Bridgette L. Threat * Minister Dunia Kambon-Thornton * Terry Wedlock * Dr. Toyia K. Younger **

On behalf of my co-authors and myself, we hope you will find healing, hope, and restoration and have a sincere and fruitful encounter with the Father.

May the Lord Bless you and protect you.

May the Lord Smile on You and be gracious to you.

May the Lord show you his favor
And give you his peace.

Numbers 6:24-26 (NLT)

~Cynthia Knight

Psalms 3:3

"But thou, O LORD, *art* a shield for me; my glory, and the lifter up of mine head."

Jeremiah 33:3

"Call unto me, and I will answer thee, and shew thee great and mighty things, which thou knowest not."

King James Version (KJV)

HEALING AND RESTORATION

Jehovah-Rapha My Healer

"The righteous cry out, and the Lord hears them; he delivers them from all their troubles. The Lord is close to the brokenhearted and saves those who are crushed in spirit." – Psalm 34:17-18

Dear Heavenly Father, I come to you as humbly as I know how just to say thank you. God, I thank you because you are God and God alone and you don't need any help. I thank you because you are my present help and if I were to search all over, I wouldn't be able to find anyone like you. God, I come to you today asking for healing of our land, healing for our nation and our people. God, I know you to be Jehovah-Rapha, my healer. So, I ask that you heal our world from all sickness and disease, heal our land from gun violence and wars between nations, heal our land from all malicious political intentions and replace it with love and a mindset to do what is right for all people whatever the background or color.

God, I ask that you see about our nation called America and heal the broken hearts of parents who have lost children to the gun violence happening all across our country. God heal minds from mental disease and bodies from any impurities within. Cause all of our limbs to operate fully the way You have created them to.

God, I pray that your people who are called by your name seek your face and turn from their wicked ways. I pray that those of us you have called rise up and take our rightful place in your kingdom to do whatever it is you have called us to do. God, I pray that you heal all of our hearts from any negativity so that we are emptied out fully receiving everything you have for us. Heal us from all past hurts, so they no longer hinder us from living fully for You and walking in the fulness of our calling.

God, heal our families and break every generational curse and stronghold so that we may never be bound again. God, heal us from the crowns of our heads to the soles of our feet, so we can be free from the enemy. Take the scales from our eyes so we are no longer blinded by the tricks and the traps that the enemy has set and will set. God, give us a heart of worship and an attentive ear to your words, your will, and your way. Give us power and increase our strength. God, we praise You even now for the exceedingly and abundantly You are going to do and for the healing that will take place all over this world. Thank you, Jehovah-Rapha. It is in Jesus name I pray, Amen!

~Minister Angelique M. Bullock

Restore Me Lord

Lord, we thank you for this opportunity to give you honor for giving us the ability to see our need to be restored in you. We thank you that we rely on your goodness to desire repentance according to Romans 2:4. Therefore, in my repentant state, I can fully understand that you desire for me to prosper and be in good health even as my soul prospers according to 3 John 2, and I cannot fulfill this promise if I am living in brokenness and condemnation.

I ask you now to release me from past guilt, shame, and trauma that causes me to live beneath my privilege in you. I acknowledge that whom You have set free is free indeed and I have no reason to be ashamed. I believe everything I have been through will work out and be used for my good, which includes bad and evil situations according to Romans 8:28.

I realize the things you are restoring me from will add joy to my days in exchange for the sorrow I have experienced. I thank you that you will give me a greater testimony to impact the kingdom now and for the years to come. My joy will be fulfilled. My life will be renewed, refreshed, and restored because I accept the liberty that comes with salvation. I am no longer a slave to my past and will honor you as Lord all the days of my life. I will cling to my knowledge that you do all things well and will reveal the purpose of my trial in due time. I will wait on you and be confident in knowing you have begun a good work in me and you will continue to perform it until Christ's return according to Philippians 1:6. In the name of Jesus I pray, amen.

~Terralyn Frazier

Power to Heal and Restore

Jehovah most high God, I come before you, asking for your power to restore. God, I'm asking that you restore broken relationships, broken promises, broken hearts, broken dreams and aspirations and the irregular health issues of your people. God, I am asking for your power to heal and restore. Your Word says in Isaiah 40:31 "They that wait upon the Lord will renew their strength. They shall mount up on wings as eagles: they shall run and not be weary: and they shall walk and not faint. So, God, I am asking you to restore strength to your people.

God, you said in your Word that if we cry out to you that you will answer. God, your children are crying out for you to do what you do best: bring restoration to our dead situations. God, whatever it may, I ask that you minister to your people individually. God, I ask that you restore those with chemical imbalances. Those whose mental illness is so debilitating that they are not able to get out of bed. God, I speak life to every situation that seems desolate and unredeemable. For we know that you are God alone, and besides you, there is no other.

God, I know that you are able to do exceedingly, abundantly above all that we can ask for and or think according to the power that is at work in us. God, I'm asking for you to send your power. God, send your power to not only restore, but to save, heal and deliver. God, I'm asking for you to show yourself mighty and strong. God, I know you are a God of restoration, and you are a God that brings life to dead situations.

God, I am trusting and believing in you to restore brokenness. God, I'm believing in you to restore families. God, I'm believing you to restore broken hearts. God, I'm believing you to restore broken relationships. God, I am asking you to restore health. God, I'm asking you to fix hearts. God, I'm asking you to regulate minds. For I know you to be a doctor in a sickroom. God, I know you to be a lawyer in the courtroom. God, I know you to be all that I need and then some! I ask all of these things in the precious name of Jesus. Amen

~Minister Dunia Kambon-Thornton

THE MASTER'S TOUCH

Introduction:

March 2020, I was hospitalized. The doctors said congestive heart failure. My heart was functioning at fifty percent capacity. I trust God for healing what he creates. I trust him for giving the doctors knowledge. And I trust his ability to heal. Today my heart is functioning. I am believing His word to be continuously manifested.

Prayer:

Almighty God, I believe your word is true, and your promise to heal assured. I thank you for your power to heal. Your word declares that you are the God that health (Exodus 15:26). By the stripes of your Son, your Word manifested in flesh, I receive your healing. I believe your word to manifest its power for those experiencing emotional and or physical challenges. Even amid a global pandemic, I have seen the result of your healing touch. You can heal what You create.

Our physical wellbeing, our emotional wellbeing, and our spiritual wellbeing is in Your healing hands: our hearts, our bodies, and our souls. Your word also declares that it is your desire that I prosper and be in good health as our soul prospers. I stand in Your promise and your manifested power to heal for myself and others. I stand in testimony of your power. I ask that you touch those in need of you. For there is nothing beyond the scope of your power. These things I pray in Jesus' name. Amen.

~Reverend Darryl D. Brookins

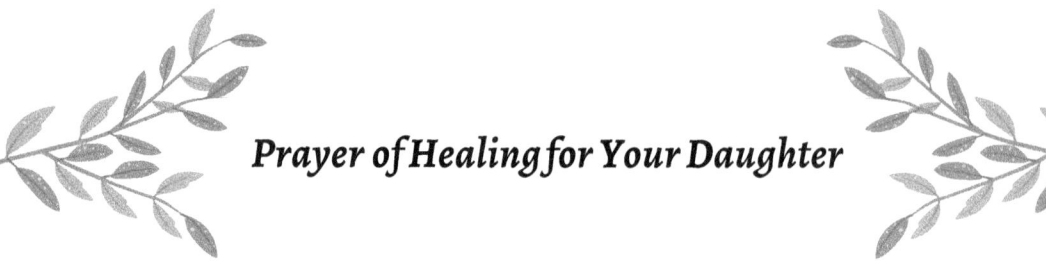

Prayer of Healing for Your Daughter

Jehovah God, in the name of Jesus, I come to you weary and worn.

Lord, I have a child that has an affliction that I don't understand.

Lord, my faith has wavered in this matter, so Lord forgive me for not understanding what to do.

Lord forgive me for allowing the enemy to show me the way of the world.

Lord see me through the blood of Jesus.

Lord, invoke the angels that are assigned to my daughter. Cover her and keep her.

Lord let no hurt, harm, or danger come to her.

Lord cover the doctors who are over her care. Show them Lord that you are the ultimate provider and that you will take care of her.

Lord strengthen those around her. Strengthen me, Lord.

Just as Abraham was obedient and was willing to sacrifice Isaac, Lord put a ram in the bush for me.

But if it's Your will Lord that this affliction takes her life, Lord strengthen me so that it becomes acceptable to me that you loaned my daughter to me for just a little while.

Lord, I know you will show up in this season to show people who you are.

I trust your will and your way Lord.

Keep us in perfect peace as we wait Lord.

Let us not lack for anything, Father God.

We love you Father.

Amen.

~Cassandra Epps

Healing Is the Children's Bread

He himself bore our sins in his body on the tree, that we might die to sin and live to righteousness. By his wounds you have been healed. Pet. 2:24

Right now, in the name of Jesus, I pray for healing and wholeness of those reading this prayer. I call on Jehovah Rapha to move in and through this prayer, bringing healing to every reader and hearer, in the name of Jesus.

I pray for order and alignment to take place in the circulatory and cardiovascular system, that the blood would flow freely through the veins, arteries, and heart normally, I command that clots dissolve, blood pressure and sugar levels be stabilized. Let all valves operate consistently and correctly. Let there be no clogs or blockages, no swelling or shrinkage in the heart, arteries or veins, in the name of Jesus.

I pray for health in the digestive and excretory system, that the stomach would break down food in the proper manner and the intestines would function as intended. I plead the blood of Jesus against acid reflux, GERD, irritable bowel syndrome, polyps, boils, tumors, cysts, hemorrhages, blockages, obstructions, and any other ailments occurring, and I command them to be nullified now in the name of Jesus.

I pray for the immune system and plead the blood of Jesus against autoimmune diseases, those illnesses that would cause the body to turn on itself and attack other systems in the body.

Jehovah Rapha bring healing to lupus, rheumatoid arthritis, celiac, Crohn's disease, ulcerative colitis, thyroiditis, hyperthyroidism, psoriasis, multiple sclerosis, and Addison's disease. Lord heal your people from bloodborne pathogens, HEP-C, HEP-B & HIV/AIDS, be dispelled now in the name of Jesus.

I pray for the renal and urinary system and come against urinary tract infections, bladder infections, kidney failure, dialysis, kidney stones, or anything that would impair the body from eliminating waste as it should, in the name of Jesus.

I speak healing in the respiratory system and pray that the lungs would absorb oxygen and dispel carbon dioxide as they should. The blood of Jesus be against asthma, bronchitis, COPD, pneumonia, and cancer.

I pray for emotional healing, healing in the conscious mind and the subconscious mind. Lord bring healing to those suffering with depression, anxiety, panic attacks, phobias, obsessive-compulsive disorder, bipolar, schizophrenia and PTSD. Do what only you can Jehovah Rapha for your people in the name of Jesus.

I come against all polyps, growths, ulcers, boils, abscesses, tumors, cysts and cancers and command them to dry up, shrink and disintegrate now by the power of the name of Jesus. Let all bodily fluids, functions and systems come into proper alignment and function as divinely intended by the power of the Holy Spirit and in Jesus' mighty name. Amen.

~Elder Elect Sonja Owens

Power Over Rejection

God, I come to you on behalf of those who struggle with rejection. Those who have been rejected by their family, job, friend, or lover. God, I ask that you comfort them as only you can. God, I know you to be the Great Comforter and you that with you, all things are possible. God, I ask that you allow them to feel your loving arms around them. God, surround them with your love, your joy, your peace, your hope, your strength, your power and your tenacity. God, I ask that you allow your Word to provide divine strength in their time of need. God, I ask that you help them to find acceptance through you. God, although people have rejected them, let them know that you would never walk away. Help them to know how much you love them. Show them through your Word that you will never leave them or forsake them. God, I ask that you show them that you are God of all and that you do all things well. God, although they feel abandoned, show them that you promise to be with us even until the end of time. God, allow them to find solace in your love and your grace. I bind and rebuke any unseen force of evil that plans to come against your will for them. I speak against any friendships or relationships that are positioned against your plan for their life. God, I ask that you continue to keep and protect them from anything that is not like you. God, I love you, adore you and honor you. In the name of Jesus, I pray Amen.

~Minister Dunia Kambon-Thornton

By The Stripes of Jesus, I Am Healed

Hebrews 4:16; 3 John 2; Psalms 103:2-3; I Peter 2:24; Isaiah 53:5 Exodus 23:25; Matthew 16:19; Isaiah 54:17; Proverbs 4:20, 21; I Corinthians 6:15

Father, I come boldly before Your throne of grace to obtain help and strength for healing in my body. You said that You desire above all things that we would prosper and be in good health. Therefore, I declare I have good health. You instructed us not to forget the benefits You have given us as children of God. For You said that You would forgive us our sins and iniquities, and You would heal us of our sickness and diseases. Therefore, I receive the blessings and benefits of my healing.

I thank You Father, for sending Your word to heal and deliver me from all my destructions. Your word tells us that You are the God that heals us of all our sickness and diseases. I confess that by the stripes of Jesus, I am healed. Father, You said that You would take sickness and disease away from us. I thank You for healing me of this infirmity from my body.

I thank You Father, for the authority You have given me in Christ Jesus. With that authority, I bind every spirit of sickness and disease. I lose wholeness in the name of Jesus. I decree and declare that I am healed from the crown of my head to the sole of my feet. I thank You Father, that no weapon formed against my body or life shall prosper.

Father, I give attention to Your words, and incline my ear to your sayings. I will not let them depart from my sight but keep them in my heart, for they are my life and health to my whole body. I know that my body is the temple of Your Holy Spirit, who dwells in me. Help me to fully understand this truth so that I will keep my temple clean and healthy.

Father, as I have prayed Your Word, I thank You that it will not return to You void, but it will accomplish that which You sent it to perform. Again, I confess by the stripes of Jesus, I am healed!

In the name of Jesus I pray, amen.

God's Promise to Heal

Heal me, O Lord, and I shall be healed;
save me, and I shall be saved,
for You are my praise.
Jeremiah 17:14

I will restore health to you and heal you of your
wounds. " says the Lord.
Jeremiah 30:17

~Bridgette L. Threat

NEW BEGINNINGS

O Lord, Our Lord, how majestic is Your name in all the earth. Jehovah Rapha, Lord of healing, we thank you for your healing. You are the great physician, and heal Lord, you heal every kind of diseases. There is nothing too hard for you. We know you gave us the leaves and trees for our healing. Healing resides in you. You opened the eyes of the blind. You told the lame to pick up their bed and walk. You raised the dead. Lord, you healed the woman with the issue of blood.

Lord, you healed the woman that was bent for 18 years with a spirit of the infirmity. We ask for you to heal all sorts of cancer, hypertension, diabetes, kidney diseases, bow disorder, and all manner of sickness and disease. Jehovah Rapha, you are the God who heals. There is nothing impossible for you. Lord, you make the impossible possible. You are our healer. Lord, I pray for the physical, mental, social, emotional and the spiritual healing of your people. I pray that You would reach down and touch us and bring healing in our home and lives. Lord, remove the scales off our eyes so we can see you clearer. Open our eyes to Your truth and give us a longing to be healed from our spiritual sickness. Adonai, we ask that you touch our bodies with your healing power. Fill us with the power to heal others. Give us rest and relief from any and all pain. There's nothing that you can't heal, O God. We know all things are possible for you. You continue to blow my mind doing the things other deemed impossible. We thank you for all you do in the lives of your people. Lord, we give you all the honor, glory, and praises that are due to your name. O God, we just thank you. O God, we bless and praise your holy name. O GOD how we love you. God, we honor you , we praise you and we thank you for the things that you are doing in the lives of your people. Jehovah Rapha, we thank you for new beginnings. You said anyone in Christ is a new creature. Give us a new mind and new behaviors so that we walk and talk like you. We ask for healing from old ways, thoughts and patterns, not like you. Heal us and set us free. In Jesus' Name, Amen.

~Minister Melissa Powell-Harrell

Prayer for Recovery - I Shall Recover All!

I will give you back your health and heal your wounds," says the LORD. Jeremiah 30:17 NLT

Yet what we suffer now is nothing compared to the glory he will reveal to us later. Romans 8:18 NLT

Kind Father in Jesus' name, I come at this moment first thanking you for survival. The fact that I have lived through a pandemic is significant, at times beyond my own understanding. I am mindful that this is due to no goodness of my own. Therefore, I say Thank You!

Lord, I pray for those who are battling for their health. Many have been to the brink of death, but you have kept them alive. Now I ask, according to Jeremiah 30:17, that you restore their health and heal their aches and pains. I align my faith with their faith and ask you for a complete and full recovery. I proclaim wholeness over your children in the name of Jesus. We will not be broken, but we shall be healthy and whole!

I pray for the ones who survived Covid-19 but are now dealing with residual effects in their bodies. Father, just as you spared them from death, you are able to heal them and do it completely. I call every organ into alignment with its original purpose. I pray that every muscle will function properly. Father, I ask you to return strength to brittle bones and normalize blood flow, heart rates, and various levels within the body. Just as you have bound the death angel on behalf of your children, God, we pray that you bind spirits of infirmity and disease. I ask that you make your people well again. Please cause your people to thrive again.

As we recover, I pray that you touch the minds of your people. I ask that you renew our minds, Lord, we are mindful that you did not allow us to go through this for nothing. We recognize that there is purpose even in painful seasons. Therefore, we ask you to reveal yourself to us. Eliminate stale mindsets and negative thought patterns.

God, we do not want to live with a defeatist mentality. Give us the mentality of victory. Cause us to recover in every area of our lives. We will lack nothing because you are Jehovah Jireh, the God who provides for us!

Remind us that Romans 8:28 yet applies to our lives. All of this is working together for our good. On the days when we question you and get down on ourselves, help us remember that these afflictions do have a far more exceeding weight in glory.

Lord, I pray that you reveal your glory to us. As we recover, we commit to talk differently and walk differently. We vow not to charge you foolishly or get angry with you because of what we have gone through. We purpose to proceed with hearts full of thanksgiving and mouths filled with praises on our lips. This is our prayer, in Jesus' name, Amen!

~Evangelist Teraleen R. Campbell

THE POWER OF THE BLOOD OF JESUS

Revelations 12:11-

And they overcame him by the blood of the lamb and by the word of their testimony: and they loved not their lives unto the death".

We thank you for the Cross of Calvary and the precious blood of Jesus Christ.

We thank you that because of the blood of Jesus, we are cleansed, healed, and made whole, and we declare that we overcame the enemy by his blood.

Let the blood quicken all that is dead within us. Let the blood of Jesus re-energize, revitalize, and revive all dead potentials and spiritual gifts with in.

Through the blood of Jesus, I decree and declare that old things are passed away in our lives and are transformed to become new.

According to 1 Peter 2:24, by his stripes we were healed.

Therefore, through the blood of Jesus Christ, every system of our bodies are blessed:

- Our cardiovascular systems are blessed
- Our endocrine systems are blessed
- Our nervous systems are blessed
- Our muscular systems are blessed
- Our digestive systems are blessed
- Our respiratory systems are blessed
- Our renal systems are blessed
- Our lymphatic systems are blessed
- Our integumentary systems are blessed
- Our skeletal systems are blessed

- Our reproductive systems are blessed
- Our immune systems are blessed and effectively fights against the Covid virus and its variations.

Through the blood, we are confident dear Jesus, that you will help us, protect us and provide for us.

We are confident through the blood of Jesus that we will fulfill our God-given purposes and show forth the glory of Almighty God in the Earth.

Now through the authority of the blood, let the fire of disgrace fall upon demonic prophets assigned against our lives.

And we decree and declare that we walk in victory and claim supernatural success. In the mighty name of Jesus we pray, amen.

~ Pastor P.M. Finley

HOPE

Conversations with God: Refuge

God is our refuge and strength, an ever-present help in trouble. Psalm 46:1

Elohim Machase Lanu, God of my Refuge, I thank You for being my safe haven when the storms in my life arise, arid trouble is all around me. When I looked around and could only see darkness, You Lord, have been my light and glimmer of home in the darkness. You have kept me when I felt like I was alone in this world. Lord, I thank you for not being a man, that You should lie, nor the son of many that you should repent. Instead, you are faithful and you are true to your word. You said that you would never leave me, nor forsake me, and when I feel like I have nowhere to go, and that there is nobody I can turn to… nobody who I can trust, I can always run to you. You are my place of comfort, Lord. You are my place of joy. You are my place of peace. You are my refuge of love. When I feel forsake; You are there. When I feel rebuked, You are there. When I feel forgotten, You are there. God, when my heart grows weary, and it's filled with despair, remind me that you are there with me and for me, with your arms wide open, just waiting for me to cast my cares on you because you care for me. Thank You, Lord. My prayer is that if anyone else finds themselves alone and in despair, your faithfulness and your love will come to their remembrance and that their refuge can be found in you. Lord, be their strength when all hope is gone. Be their rock, their protector, and their safe haven. Be their light in the darkness Father… guide them back to you. Thank you, Elohim Machase Lanu, God of my Refuge. Amen!

~Minister Michelle Lee

God's My Protection

This prayer is a prayer of Protection to assist the reading in overcoming the attacks of the enemy through weapons and words. It is also to remind the reader of the power and victory that belongs to them.

Lord, I thank You for access to Your Throne. God, I thank You for access to Your listening ear in accordance with Is. 65:24. Which states, "Even before they call, I will answer; while they are still speaking, I will hear." Thank You for hearing and answering me today.

Lord, I lift up the person that is reading this prayer now. I pray that the peace of God rest, rule and abide in their lives in a supernatural way. I pray that it would be peace that surpasses even their own understanding, according to Phil. 4:6.

I frustrate, dismantle, tear apart and cause to cease and desist every work of the enemy in your life. For no weapon formed against you is able to prosper and every tongue that rises against you in judgement will he condemned, for it is your heritage according to Is. 54:17, in the name of Jesus.

I pray that a supernatural fortress of protection would cover them, their family, home, car, and everything concerning them in the name of Jesus. I dispatch warrior angels to encamp round about them and protect them from dangers seen and unseen.

Let them be hidden under your wings, for your promises are their armor and protection according to Ps. 91:4. Let Your protection encamp round about them and their family as a fortress God so that the enemy cannot track or trace them, in the name of Jesus.

I declare and decree that you are more than a Conqueror, in accordance with Rom. 8:37. Jehovah Nissi is your Banner, and therefore, protection and victory are always your portion, in the name of Jesus. Amen.

~Elder Elect Sonja Owens

For Confidence

Father God,

As I go forth today, I go forth in the power of Your might. I thank You that I am the head and not the tail; that I am above and not beneath; that greater are You that is within me, than he that is in the world. Lord, I thank You that I have the mind of Christ and that you have given me hinds feet for high places. While I may not always understand Your ways, give me faith to trust Your plan and strength to walk this road knowing that You have ordered my steps. Remove all fear, doubt, and shame, and remind me that it is in You that I live, move and have my being. Give me the confidence and boldness to go forth today in the power of Your might. Guard my tongue and bridle my lips, that I may speak the word only and not be a vessel used to tear others down. Give me the strength and tenacity to face anything the enemy throws my way, knowing that no weapon formed against me shall prosper. Show Yourself strong and might in all that I do. Father, I decrease so that you can increase and have full control over my life. I surrender my thoughts and desires for Yours. Send me daily reminders that in this world of uncertainty, you are still in control. Help me not lose the faith but become stronger in my walk with You each and every day. This day I command my morning and declare that this is the day that You have made, and I will rejoice and be glad in it. Regardless of what I see or may think, I know you are my sustainer and the lifter of my head; so I go forth in You knowing that You have already made a way. In Jesus name, I pray.

Amen

~Dr. Toyia K. Younger

Jesus' Promise:
Invite the Holy Spirit into Your life

Matthew 24:4; John 4:24; Luke 12:12

The Holy Spirit comes into our lives as the answer to Jesus' promise to send him to help us in our Christian Life. His purpose is to help us in our weaknesses, to encourage, to advocate, to comfort, to counsel, and to console. He is called to be at the side of each of us however, we have to invite Him in.

Prayer:

Father God, I thank You for the gift of the Holy Spirit. I ask You to stir up within me the fullness of Your Holy Spirit, help me to grow in my relationship with Him, to live in His power, and use His gifts.

Holy Spirit, come, fill my heart with the fire of Your love. Fill me with Your strength today. I pray that you give me a deeper level of wisdom and discernment. Be my eyes and ears so that no one may deceive me. I desire to experience Your power Holy Spirit. Lead me to grow and know about Christ and to have a deeper personal relationship with Jesus.

With a willing heart, Holy Spirit, I invite you into my life. Jesus said, "God is Spirit, and those who worship Him must worship in spirit and truth." Without You, I cannot worship God in spirit and in truth. Without You Holy Spirit, I cannot live a righteous and faithful life. Holy Spirit, thank You for always being there, thank You for always waiting patiently for me to call on You. Help me to never grieve You Holy Spirit by resisting Your call or neglecting You.

Thank you, Holy Spirit, for your presence with me, flowing freely in and through me. Thank You for being my resting place. Thank You for being my friend, my teacher, my comforter, my counselor, and my intercessor.

In the name of Jesus I pray, amen

God's Promise to Send the Holy Spirit

If you love me, you will obey what I command And I will ask the Father, and he will give you another Counsellor to be with you forever - the Spirit of truth. The world cannot accept him, because it neither sees him nor know him. But You know him, for he lives with you and will be in you. John 14:15-17

But I tell you the truth; It is for your good that I am going awry. Unless 1 go away, the Counsellor will not come to you; but if I go, I will send him to you John 16:7.

~Bridgette L. Threat

Conversations with God: Protection

But you Lord, are a shield around me, my glory, the one who lifts my head high. Psalm 3:3

Elohim Shomri, God my Protector, I greet you today with a sincere heart of gratitude because there has never been a time in my life when you were not there for me; Blessing me, keeping me, covering me with your Grace, your mercy, your faithfulness, your favor and your love. You know all about me, Lord, and you understand the matters of my heart. When my enemies have gathered to cause me harm, you were right there shielding me from their fiery darts. When tongues wagged against me, you exposed the naysayers and silenced their noise. When I was falsely accused, you vindicated me, and you made my enemies, my footstools. When I was in harm's way, you had your angels encamped around me. Father, your hedge of protection has been ever-present in my life, even when I didn't know that I needed it.

Lord, I thank you for that because I realize that there are times when I am unknowingly shielded from hurt, harm and danger, and you rescue me and keep me protected. Father, I am grateful to be able to stand on your promises and to know that I can trust your Word. You are my refuge and my fortress, my God in whom I trust. (Psalm 91:16) I stand in gratitude today because I know that weapons may form, but they will not prosper against me (Isaiah 54:17), for I know how to call on the Name of The Lord when I need help. The Name of the Lord is a strong tower, the righteous run to it and is safe. (Proverbs 18:10) Thank you, Lord, for the safety and protection that is found only in you. Thank you for being my shield, my glory and the lifter of my head; in Jesus' Name I pray, Amen!

~ Minister Michelle Lee

PRAISE and THANKS

In Your Presence

Lord, I come to you with great praise and thanks. Your loving kindness towards me is unmatched. You are the Lover of my soul. The Keeper of my heart. The Provider for my journey. The Sustainer of my way. Today God, I am pouring out my gratitude. Thank you for being faithful and never leaving me. Lord, I bless you for allowing me to have an audience with you whenever I desire. You never turn me away. You are never too busy to answer when I call Your Name. You turn back time to restore what the locust and the cankerworm have taken from me and allow me to recover it all. Hallelujah! The best is what You desire for me and that you will never withhold. What a Gracious God! Daily, I desire to be in Your presence. Safe from all harm. Protected from every ill motive. Lacking nothing. Able to lay all this world's troubles down at your feet. Oh Lord, I thank you for this place of safety. In your presence, I gain Your mind. Your character. I am cleansed of all unrighteousness. Gaining purity of thought. My spirit is aligned with Yours. The more I commune with You and sup at your table, you become my primary focus. To glean from your infinite Wisdom and become more like You is what I purpose to accomplish. There is a grace that comes upon me in your presence. I need you, Holy Spirit. Lead and guide me into the place You predestined before the foundation of the world. Take me there. I am there. In Jesus Name, Amen.

~Nicki Nichols

Lord, We Trust You

2 Chronicles 20:22

And when they began to sing and to praise, the Lord set ambushes against the children of Ammon, Moab, and mount Seir, which were come against Judah; and they were smitten.

God WILL fight our battles! If you find yourself in the fight of your life! And you are out of strength, find Joy in knowing you are not out of God! His strength is made perfect in our weakness. Lord, we focus on the tools you gave us to be like King Jehoshaphat and defeat this enemy! We believe you are sending ambushes on our behalf... let us pray!

Lord, it's again we say thank you! Thank you, Lord, for this great and powerful vehicle called prayer we GET to share with you! Thank you for the intimacy, thank you for the truth of your word, thank you, Lord, that you are ever near and that you deal kindly with us! Lord, we stand here facing a great challenge!

Lord, we feel this is the fight of our lives... and I'm this time we are reminded that in the days when King Jehoshaphat had 3 vast armies marching against them, and they were afraid. They were outnumbered and didn't see how they could possibly win this one. Lord, we feel pressed down on every side. We feel shaken! But we take our brother in Christ example here, and we do as the King did, we turn to you in prayer. We place our trust AND hope fully in you, in the TRUTH of your word. No solution we can come up with will suffice or be sufficient to get us through, so God, we are leaning on the arms of grace and mercy!

Lord, be our anchor during this most difficult time! Lord, you told our brother in Christ here in this scripture to have faith and trust you, oh Lord, WE TRUST You! We know and believe that you are behind the scenes working on our behalf. We are going to refocus our fight. The king didn't go into battle with his own might Lord, and neither do we! Instead, we put on a spirit of PRAISE! We come into this spiritual fight with a song on our heart and a praise on our lips of thanksgiving! We are thanking you for fighting on our behalf. We are thanking you for making a way, we are thanking you for getting us this far by faith! We don't believe you have taken us THIS far to leave us, Lord! We speak LIFE to every grave situation we see because, Lord, we believe just as you did for King Jehoshaphat, you are fighting and sending ambushes on our behalf!

We believe in the power, your power Lord! We believe that you reign. We give you praise for being the author and finisher of our faith! In you Lord do we move and have our very being! Nothing is too hard for you. You are well able AND willing to help us in our time of need! Your word declares that you are a VERY PRESENT help in the time of trouble! We call out for your HELP today! Oh Lord, We cancel premature death from the fight! We speak Life! Oh God, you have called us to LIVE, and we shall LIVE and not die!

Oh Lord, as we pray this prayer, revive broken hearts, sick and stricken bodies, fill us up with your Holy Spirit, oh God reign down on us so that we can produce Glory for you in such a way that it makes you smile! We Lord your people what to make you smile!!!! Here is our life, Lord, USE US father for your glory! We say Yes, Lord! Thank you in advance for defeating our enemies.

Thank you that you cause us to win! Thank you that the enemy remains defeated in our lives in the name of Jesus! Thank you that you hear our prayer, and not only do you hear our prayers, God, that you always do something about them! Hallelujah! We praise you. We will not allow the enemy to stifle our praise because our praise is a weapon, and even if we have to pry open our own mouths, we refuse to allow the rocks to cry out on our behalf! We will praise you a lord FOREVER in the bad and good times, we cancel the spirit of fear and doubt, and we speak life! We declare we are overcomers in Jesus name! And we believe it to be so, Amen!

~Renee Myers

Thank you, Lord

Lord, I thank you for today. Each day on earth is a gift, and I am truly grateful. Many times, I come to you in prayer with requests, but right now, I just want to honor and bless your name and acknowledge that I owe everything to You! I am nothing without you. You are my source, my help, my listening ear, my comfort, my motivator - Lord, you are my everything! I thank you for being omnipotent (all powerful), omnipresent (everywhere) and omniscient (all-knowing). You know my every thought before it forms, my words before I speak and my actions before I move, and still, you love me.

Thank you for loving me unconditionally-through my disobedience, arrogance, sin, and filthiness. You didn't judge me. Instead, you invited me to come to you, just as I was. Thank you, God, for the opportunity to erase my sin, my shame, my ungodliness. Thank you for reminding me that I am a King's child, I am wonderfully made, and I am new through You. I am honored to call you my Father!

Thank you, God, for peace. With the flurry of activity in our world - Hurricanes and Earthquakes, Social Injustice, COVID 19, Political Unrest and Evacuation efforts in Afghanistan - it is very easy to feel overwhelmed, depressed or even helpless, but Lord, I thank you for peace. You are my rock and fortress when it feels like life is caving in on me. You are my sounding board, my comfort, my confidante, and my guiding light. I may not feel it right away, but God, the more I say it, the more it comes to fruition. We must seek peace and pursue it {Psalms 34:14). Thank you, Lord, for providing something that no one else can and something that money cannot buy-thank you for peace.

Lord, I give you the highest praise - Hallelujah! Thank you for everything, and thank you for being my God!

~Amanda B. Sumiel

Thank You, Father

Dear Heavenly Father,

Thank you for this day that you have made. I rejoice, and I am glad in it. You've granted me new mercies today, and I look forward to seeing the mighty works of your hands. I thank you that you are the God of all creation, and without you, there is nothing made that was made. I thank you that you are with me, and you have never left me nor forsaken me, and you promise to stay with me till the end of the age.

Thank you that you are a very present help in trouble. Thank you for being a strong tower and my place of refuge. Thank you for allowing me to enter your rest. Thank you for supplying all my needs. Thank you that goodness and mercy are following me all the days of my life. Thank you for your love that surpasses all understanding. Thank you for giving me all things that pertain to life and godliness. Thank you for teaching me our ways. Thank you for correcting me so that I am not walking in error, and which lets me know that I am your son. Thank you for your word that is a lamp unto my feet and a light unto my path. Thank you that you are not a man that you would lie and that I can put all my trust in you. Thank you that I know Jesus is the truth, the light and the way. Thank you for your promises that are yes and amen. Thank you that your word will not return to you void, that it will accomplish what you purpose it to do. Thank you for breath in my body and another day to pursue after you, another day to worship you, another day to come into your presence. Thank you for comforting me and strengthening me. Thank you for making me more than a conqueror through Christ Jesus, who strengthens me. Thank you that no weapon formed against me will prosper. Thank you for truth!

Thank you for providing me with an understanding of your word. Thank you for wisdom. Thank you for loving me so much that you gave your only begotten son, Jesus Christ, to be the propitiation for my sins. Thank you for the gift of salvation. Thank you for giving me the power to become a son of God. Thank you that when this journey is over in this lifetime, I will look like Christ. Thank you for creating a new heaven and a new earth where I will serve you forever and ever. Thank you for choosing me.

~Mya Jackson Brown

EVERYTHING I NEED:

(In reference order): Isaiah 59:1; Number 14:34; Genesis 21:9; 1 Kings 18:27, Psalm 121:4; Psalm 147:3; Lamentations 3:22-23; Hosea 2:15; 1 Peter 2:9; Philippians 4:19; Exodus 20:2, Psalm 86:5, Matthew 6:25; Psalms 55:22, 1 John 1:9; Genesis 17:1.

Father, I thank You for being the God who sees and the God who hears! Thank You for being *my* God who cares for *me*. You are with me when I find myself in a wilderness-whether I have wandered on my own volition like Your children of Israel or rejected and sent like Your daughter Hagar-You are here!

Thank You for not being a God who sleeps, who shuts its eyes and covers its ears when there is a cry for help. Thank You for being *my* God, the Everlasting Father, who tends to my cries, binds up my wounds and heals me when I am broken. Thank You for being a Father who is full of Loving kindness and tender mercies. You take pleasure in bestowing them upon Your children every day because You are faithful and moved with compassion. *You* are God. Your arm reaches to the highest of mountains and flows to the lowest of valleys to rescue me out of darkness. Even in my personal Valley of Achor, You are my hope!

Thank You for snatching me out of this dark place and returning me to Your marvelous Light! It is *here* that I find my daily bread. E-ver-y-thing I need is in You. Again, I say thank You because, as Your children, we can ask Your forgiveness for substituting our tears for the love You so freely give; Your forgiveness is immediate. *Forgive me* for making my tears my sustenance. In You, there are no substitutes. *You* are my sustenance-You are El Shaddai-more than enough! AMEN and AMEN!

~Elder Alicia A. Richardson

A Thankful Heart

PSALMS: 106:1

*Praise the Lord. Give thanks to the Lord, for he is good;
his love endures forever.*

Heavenly Father, I come to you to say THANK YOU! Thank you for allowing me to experience life with you. God, I am not worthy of the blessings that I have received from you, but I am thankful every morning when I open my eyes and inhale fresh air. While this may be an ordinary blessing to most, this is an extraordinary blessing to me.

Without you, I know that none of these things would be possible.

God, thank you for loving me. At my best and especially at my worse. Thank you for never taking your hand off me. Thank you for accepting me at my least and at times. when I was the hardest to love. Thank you for sending amazing people to me on my journey. Thank you for a wonderful family and an abundance of friends. Thank you for allowing me to see the value that each one has played in my life so far. Thank you for allowing me to see people through your eyes. Thank you for reminding me daily that everyone has something unique to offer to the world.

God, thank you for peace. Your peace surpasses all understanding. Challenges arise in life, but with GOD's peace, I know that I will get through anything that life throws my way. Thank You for being an incredible father. You are all-knowing and all-wise. You are a fervent protector. You have protected me from myself as well as dangers seen and unseen.

God, thank you for joy. It took years for me to learn that joy comes from you alone, not from a perfect circumstance but from a perfect GOD. Pure joy is found in the smallest, most ordinary blessings.

God, thank you for being omnipotent, omnipresent, and omniscient. Your power, your presence, and your knowledge have impacted my life in the most unimaginable ways. Your plans for my life look completely different from mine, and for that alone, I am grateful. My imagination will never measure up to your blessings. Thank You, God, for exceeding expectations and blessing me in both ordinary and extraordinary ways.

God, thank you for these things. God, this prayer is a Thank You for you being who you are. Thank you for loving me enough to keep blessing me in ways that I have not seen nor can dream. Thank you for everything, God. AMEN.

~Toni G. Guy

A Prayer of Thanksgiving

Lord, I thank You for just being our God. I thank You for Your mercy, Your loving kindness, and Your long suffering with mankind. We owe you so much, and You only ask for a repentant heart. A life that would perpetuate holiness and manifest Your Name in the earth. You are a Holy God that deserves a holy people.

Lord, You alone are our sustainer of life. All blessings flow from above. Thank You for Your protection in bringing us through the plague and pestilence in the land. You bring peace in dark times of turmoil and oppression and feelings of depression. Thank You for the deliverance from the enemy's attack on our health and our finances. Thank You for being a prayer-answering God. Prayer gives us hope and comfort when we're doing our best but still failing in life's accomplishments. Thank You for just allowing us to put down those burdens and place them all at Your Feet. Our best, cannot compare to the <u>least</u> that you can do for us. Truly " ... Eye have not seen, nor ear heard... the things which God hath prepared for them that love him." *(I Corinthians2:9 KJV)*. Thank You, Lord, for Your goodness and Your great love. Thank You, Lord, for caring. Lord, it is Your desire that we prosper even as our soul prospers. <u>All</u> blessings flow from above.

Lord God, increase our faith to hold fast to our belief in You and show gratitude for Your many life-sustaining blessings.

Most of all, Lord, I thank You for the Son that paid a debt that "He did not owe." He paid it for us, sinful mankind; for a stubborn and unthankful generation. I want to say thank You again, Lord, for Your kindness, Your mercy and Your grace.

Dear God, we could never repay You. I thank You for the understanding we have of Your precious word, but we need more, Lord. More wisdom, knowledge and understanding. Lord, I thank You for every gift and talent that You have given us and I pray for an increase so that we are able to stand fast to do your will and exalt you throughout all the Earth.

In the Precious Name of Jesus I pray, AMEN

~Evangelist Elaine Harmon

WORSHIP and ADORATION

You Do All Things Well

"My mouth is filled with your praise, declaring your splendor all day long." – Psalm 71:8

Lord, we worship You because You do all things well. You are Alpha and Omega, beginning and the end. You are the creator God, omniscient and omnipresent. We speak nothing but Your greatness because You are worthy of all the glory, honor and praise. Nothing or no one is deserving of our worship, and God, we are sorry if our actions and words have made you think otherwise. Lord, we lift our hands and our heads today because we adore You all that you are. You are mighty, gracious, and merciful and we thank you because you didn't have to do anything, but you did. In spite of us, God, you continue to bless us, protect us, provide for us, cleanse us, fill us, keep us from dangers seen and unseen, and wrap us in Your loving arms and for that God, we worship you today.

We worship You because You order our every step and guide us on the path that you would have us to go. Even when we stray, You reel us back in with Your staff. We worship You because You rescue us over and over again and are our refuge where the righteous run in and are saved. Your power and Your love has no bounds. Although we place you in a box, You show us day in and day out that You're bigger. We worship you for all the ways you made, the ways you are currently making, and the ways you have yet to make. All praises be to the King of Kings, Glory and Honor to Your name.

We worship You for your countless miracles, and we stand in awe of You. Hallelujah to your name! We worship You for Your mighty acts and for the great strength. God, please continue to allow us to be witnesses of Your powerful works and recipients of Your blessings. Lord, we will never stop worshiping Your name. We love you, and we magnify you. In the mighty name of Jesus, at the name that every knee shall bow and every tongue shall confess that Jesus Christ is Lord, it is in that name we pray, Amen!

~Minister Angelique M. Bullock

"BE THE ONE"

God, You are our Refuge and our Strength. You went to the cross

Enduring the torment, shame and guilt of our sins, the sins of sinful man.

Who will be the one to come to You to express thanks? The one showing gratitude for You enduring the torment and shedding Your Blood. Who will turn from their wicked ways and seek to serve You? Who will be the one to thank you?

Who will seek a right relationship with God? Closer to Your will God and not our own. We owe Jesus our lives. Who will be the one to thank You? Being a sacrifice for Him is the righteous thing to do. We should willingly present our "bodies as a living sacrifice, holy and acceptable to God." * As the song writer says, "mold my heart, transform my mind and conform my will to Yours" O'LORD.

In Jesus Name AMEN

From: Walking with Mary by Edward Sri, 2013,2017

"Be The One" is a phrase that was used by the famous Catholic nun, Mother Teresa. She was a great missionary that attended to people living in poverty and with various illnesses. I cannot fully explain what the phrase meant to her. I read that after reflecting on Jesus being alone at the Cross, she posed the question, "Who would be the one" to comfort Jesus in His suffering?

This phrase inspired me to initiate this prayer, "Be The One." My focus for the prayer is that Jesus will find comfort in our faith which He says pleases Him.

~Evangelist Elaine Harmon

God of Glory

God in heaven, I come to you not asking for anything but to thank you for everything. God, I thank you for allowing us the privilege to me before you. God, I thank you that you are a relational God. I thank you, Lord, that you are a God that wants to commune with us. God, I thank you for not only all that you have done but also for what you are doing. God, I thank you for the flowers, trees, the birds and the bees. God, I come before you with adoration and thanksgiving because you are a holy and righteous God. God, I adore you because you are God alone, and beside you, there is no other. God, I adore you because you are the King of Kings and the Lord of Lords. God, I give you glory because you are the Great I AM. You are Jehovah Jireh.

You provide what we need. God, I thank you for providing food, clothing and shelter. God, I worship you because you are Jehovah Rapha. God, I thank you for your healing power. God, I thank you for being the God that heals our diseases. I thank you that you continue to heal. God, I thank you in advance for the healing of cancer, covid, diabetes, high blood pressure, mental illness, and any other disease or disorder that plagues our nation. God, I thank you because you are Jehovah Nissi. God, you are our banner. God, I thank you that you defend and protect us from all hurt, harm and danger. God, I thank you for being El Haka Bodh. You are the God of glory. God, I thank you for your glory. God, I thank you for revealing your glory to your people. God, I-thank you for your glory. God, it's your glory that will save, heal and deliver. God, I thank you for your glory. For it's in your glory where chains are broken, and the bound are freed. God, it's your glory where the supernatural breaks into the natural and lives are changed. It's in your glory where we see miracle, signs, and wonders. God release your glory into the earth. We need your glory. God, I worship you. I give you praise not just for what you can do but also for who you are. God, you are the sovereign, all-powerful Lord of all. God, I thank you that you made us in your image.·

~ Minister Dunia Kambon-Thornton

My Souls Delight

Father God,

You are mighty in all Your ways. Great is your name and You are greatly to be praised. You are a God who sits high and looks low. You cradle your children in the palm of Your hands; great is Your mercy. There is nothing too hard for You, God. In our darkest places, You are light. When we are lost and don't know which way to turn, You are a compass for our way! Thank You, Heavenly Father. Your Word is a lamp onto our feet and a light onto our paths. You love us so much that You gave Your only Son as a living sacrifice for our sins. All praises to Your Holy name. If we searched high and low and far and wide, there would be no one greater than You. No one or nothing will ever have my heart, soul or mind the way that You do, Lord. We love You so much, and we can't live without You. Please remain an ever-present help in our time of trouble. You strengthen us when we are weak and You sustain us from all hurt, harm and danger. My soul gets excited and my heart fills with joy when I think of Your goodness and mercy. Continue to bless Your children and continue to be a living presence in our lives. Father, keep us away from evil and let us draw closer to You. We seek the secret place of the Most High God and abide in the presence of the Almighty. Allow Your Holy Spirit to guide us and let us not be snared by the works of the devil. Give us discerning power to resist the temptation of the enemy and to do Your Will. Thank You, Father, that You keep us in perfect peace. We want to live boldly and confidently in Your Son, Jesus. This prayer is prayed in the precious and holy name of Your Son, Jesus Christ.

Amen

~ Minister Mishawn A. Jones

Could It Be?

Father God, trouble surrounds me on every hand.

I am afraid and the only thing I know to do is turn to you.

What is it about You God that makes you an ever-present help in the times of my storms and trouble?

Could it be that You said you would fight for me and all I must do is be still?

Could it be You said I was more than a conquer through Jesus Christ?

Could it be You gave your only begotten Son to save my wretched undeserving soul?

What is it about you God that makes you mindful of me and my circumstance?

Could it be because you are sovereign?

Could it be because you laid the earth's foundation?

Could it be because you placed the Stars and the Constellations?

Could it be because you are blame-less and no one contends with you?

You are my God and you will fight for me.

Your omnipresence surrounds me and my problems, so why should I be afraid?

Your glorious and opulent love astounds me. My soul cries Holy, Holy, Holy! Any words I offer cannot sum up your worth. They fail miserably when trying to lavish you with the honor you are due.

You are the One true God, the King of Kings, and My Great I AM, and could it be, as a reflection of you, "I am" in complete awe and absolute love with you? The answer to that question is Yes!

I am reassured when I come to you oh God, for it is never a case of could it be, but IT IS SO, and for that and so much more I will rejoice in you my God and praise your mighty name. Amen.

~Cynthia Knight

MORNING DEVOTIONALS

Morning Devotional: New Mercies

Oh, what a mighty and powerful God we serve! As I look and listen this morning, I recognize how amazing you are. The dew on the green grass, golden sunrise, and sweet sound of birds singing are just a few of your amazing creations. Today is going to be awesome! Lord, as I put my feet on the ground, I realize how blessed I am to be alive, to breath on my own accord, to rise without any aches or pains, and to walk with no assistance. As I prepare for my day, I thank you for my family and friends, my pastor and church family, a great job with an easy commute, finance, and good health. I am so blessed and have so much I am grateful for. Thank you, Lord, for everything. Every day should be a day of thanksgiving.

Lord, go with me today and help me guard my thoughts and tongue. I need your spirit to help me glorify you not only through my words but also through my actions. God, I want to be a vessel to be used to uplift your kingdom.

Thank you, God, for new mercies and grace every morning. I praise you for your covering, your protection, and your love. Thank you for supplying my needs, natural and spiritual. Sometimes, I may not receive "things" when I want them, but God will always provide what I need in His time. Thank you for spiritual food and wisdom. Thank you for your Word and for opening my heart to receive it. Let the words come off the pages and plant themselves in my heart. Help me, Lord, to be more like Jesus, more loving and kinder when others disappoint or anger me, more meek and humble when others speak well of me, more compassionate, charitable, and willing to help those in need. Lord, help me to be a living testimony of your goodness, faithfulness, and tenderness. I approach this day with expectancy and excitement. I look forward to a great day in the Lord and know that if a challenge comes my way, You are with me. Thank you, Lord, for this new day. I will rejoice and be glad in it.

~Amanda B. Sumiel

CONVERSATIONS WITH GOD: NEW DAY

This is the day the Lord has made; let us rejoice and be glad in it. Psalm 118:24

Good Morning God! Oh Lord, Our Lord, How Excellent is They Name in All The Earth. Father, I thank you for this mornings' rising and the new mercies that greeted me today. I am so grateful that the dawning of each morning brings brand new mercies. Lord, through no power of my own, I woke up this morning with full activity of my limbs, a clear mind, and a reasonable portion of my health. This gift was not given as a result of anything I've done, but because you are better than good, and Your Grace and Your Mercy abound. For that, I give You praise. Lord, I don't ever want to take any of this for granted because somewhere, there is someone who went to bed last night, and they woke up today in Glory with you.

Lord God, I am well aware that I could have been that person, so I thank you for allowing me to see this day, a day I have never seen before, nor will I ever see it again, but I will rejoice and be glad in it! I am refreshed! I am renewed! I am anticipating great things on this day. I am grateful that you are already everywhere that I will be. Father, I am open and available to you, so please use me however you see fit. This brand-new day is another opportunity for me to serve you and to be your hands and feet on earth. Father, today I am grateful to have another chance to share your light and love with others and to present the invitation and provide the opportunity for someone to ask, "what must I do to be saved?" Lord, it is my fervent prayer that no time in this day will be wasted, but instead, it will be used to glorify you in all that I do. Lord, I thank You, Lord, I Praise You, and Lord, I lift up Your name. It is in the name of Jesus that I pray, Amen.

~Minister Michelle Lee

MORNING DEVOTION: I DELIGHT IN YOU

Psalm 113:3

"From the rising of the sun to unto the going down of the same the Lord's name is to be praised."

Almighty God,

Early in the morning before the rising of the sun, I seek Your face, Lord. To be in Your presence ·is where I desire to be. The birds sing Your praises, and the morning dew quenches my thirst for You. Let there be nothing like You on my mind, in my heart or in my spirit. Crucify my flesh! Clean me of all unrighteousness and create in me a clean heart. Thank You for this day which You have made; I will rejoice and be glad in it. Father, give me my daily bread, and please provide me with what I need to make it through this day. Today is a new chance to love, give and be all that You have called me to be. Morning by morning, new mercies You give.

Show me how to live a life filled with Your Word. Let others see Your Son, Jesus in me. Thank you for allowing me to be washed in the blood of Christ. Let me not become distracted by the things of this world during this day. Protect me from self-doubt and low self-esteem. Instead, let Your love shine through me because I was created in Your image. Keep a hedge-fence of protection around me in my coming and my going. Keep me from falling, failing, and faltering in any area of my life. Bless me like only You can do, Father.

It is my desire to let others see the love, joy, peace, patience, kindness, goodness, faith, humility, and self-control that Your Spirit provides. Your presence goes out before so that no matter what comes my way, You have already conquered it, in Jesus' name. Let me not conform to this world and all of its trappings, but continue to let me be transformed daily with the renewing of my mind. Keep me inspired to be better today than I was yesterday. Let my words, thoughts, and actions be pleasing to You, Lord. Your mercy is so good, and it endures forever.

My heart smiles when I think of the fact that You delight in my seeking Your presence this morning. Let me never forget that being in Your presence is a gift, and it is not to be taken for granted. Thank You for Your angels that watch over me throughout today. I stand boldly, confidently, and steadfastly in Your Will. And I pray this in Jesus' divine name, Amen

~Minister Mishawn A. Jones

A MORNING DEVOTIONAL

Philippians 3:14 KJV

LORD, I thank you for allowing me to see another day. A day that you have made.

Another opportunity to rejoice in worship and praise to YOU. Another opportunity to reach someone with a word from You O'LORD. To draw someone ever closer to You. Lord, to encourage another to *"Press toward the mark for the prize of the high calling of God in Jesus Christ" *;· to seek the kingdom of heaven.*

I thank You for just knowing who You are and who I am **in** You, Lord.

LORD, I pray for Your continued protection throughout this day. Protection for me, for my household, and my Pastor. I ask that you remember other leaders as well who are working in the vineyard. LORD, I ask for your guidance. Direct my path so I will remain in the Path that You have chosen for me. I pray against any distractions or hindering spirits that come to destroy my purpose in the Lord's kingdom, for You alone are God Almighty. Day by day, I pray to continue to devote my life to You. That God, You remain first and foremost in my life, for You alone are God Almighty, my keeper, my protector, and sustainer of life.

LORD, please order my steps that I do not stumble along the way of my daily journey with You towards eternal life in Christ Jesus. LORD, help me to continuously walk in Your ways and not faint. I thank you, LORD, for life and the great things You've done and what You are going to do in my life.

In the Mighty Name of Jesus I pray AMEN

~Evangelist Elaine Harmon

MY DEVOTION IS TO YOU

Introduction:

I take every moment I can to offer thanks to God for all He does, for all He is, and for all He's been to me. I have found that the best way to start the day is with His name on my lips. Starting my day with Him is the best way to start the day that He has made.

Prayer:

Most High God. Thank you for this day you have given me. It is my joy to start my day with you. Thank you for granting me this day. You are the one that makes life worth living. You are the most high God. You are the Great God. There is none that stands beside you. There is no other God but you. I lift your name. I extol you for who you are. There is none greater than you.

I thank you for all that you have done in my life. I thank you for your word. Your word that brings life, your word that is life. Thank you for your provision. Thank you for life. Thank you for being my source of all that is and all that will be. You hold me in your hand. You sustain me. You maintain me. My very existence is in You. It is because of You, I am. You are the air I breathe. My life is in your hand.

~Reverend Darryl D. Brookins

GOD HELP ME, SAVE ME

A Cry For Help

Lord, I pray that our prayers reach your ears and rescue the many Who desire change in their lives. Change in their spirit man and healing of their souls to create a closer relationship with You Lord. We don't want to say, Lord, Lord, but in reality, our hearts are *far* from You.

Hear my cry, O Lord, hide us in Your Secret Place, in Your Pavilion, a covering for our souls. We need Your protection from the evil in the land, from the fiery darts of the enemy who seeks to steal our faith and destroy our lives in Christ. Protect us from the enemy that is roaming the earth seeking to devour us by robbing many of your great Love and Hope in Christ Jesus. I refuse to faint in the face of adversity, a pandemic, civil unrest, and great violence in the land. I pray for peace and a unified Body of Christ that will manifest your goodness Lord and draw others to you.

Lord, I pray that the Church will move in unity and agreement as ONE, knowing that by remaining obedient to You and trusting You, O Lord that the enemy will **not** be able to snatch us out of your Hand. I thank you, God, for Your sacrificial LOVE and Your refuge of protection of peace and of comfort.

In Jesus Name I Pray, AMEN

~Evangelist Elaine Harmon

Flawed but Not Forsaken

Lord, When I make choices that are out of your will and contrary to your thoughts towards me, I appreciate your loving correction. You chastise those whom you love because it is not your desire for us to be overtaken or led astray. I decree and declare; I will learn and grow from every situation the enemy has sent to hinder my forward movement. I release my old mind to you, Lord, and receive this new mind that is in Christ Jesus. Show me how to correct my wrongs. Break up every haughty spirit of condemnation in my life. Lead me down the narrow path of your choosing. For each relationship, financial opportunity, or daily responsibility that has been mishandled, please forgive me. Teach me how to properly appropriate every resource provided unto me, to give you Glory. I recognize that repentance, grace, and mercy are gifts from you, Father. I will enter your gates with a humble spirit and with thanksgiving, knowing you are the author and finisher of my faith. Every good work that you have started in me, you will complete it.

Therefore, I disallow the opinions of others to disqualify me for the work you have begun in my life. Deliverance from people-pleasing is what I desire. To emerge from the bondage of this action that causes stagnation, worry, doubt and fear, for you have not given your children the spirit of fear but of power, love, and a sound mind. Lord, fortify my heart to no longer desire man's approval but to rest in knowing that your approval is more than enough. Thank you, Father, for the pre-approved destiny that lies ahead. In Jesus Name, Amen.

~Nicki Nichols

God Hear My Voice

God, as I turn my face and look up to the sun and clouds above beyond the skies, please hear my voice among the many others that you hear on this realm of the earth calling your name to hear and listen to their petitions to you.

I'm just one of your many servants, children of God, and adopted children into your royal spiritual family. Who is hurting and crying out to You at all hours of the day and night, feeling alone at times and frustrated with some of the circumstances of life that I must walk through in my life's journey?

God, You are my solid and unmovable rock in my life, Lord, You are the foundation that my relationship is built upon, God, You are my refuge that I can come to for protection when I'm in distressed in any situation, when things have fallen out of order and are in disarray.

God, I have nobody to turn to but You for my help with my circumstances, for your vast and abundant knowledge and wisdom, for I confess with my heart and voice, "I cannot do this alone nor in my own power." God, I am dependent upon you just as your faithful servant Job was God to deliver me from my pain and affliction, from my long-suffering, from my loneliness, and all that I lost or that was taken from me God, by whom I don't know?

All I know is to get on my knees and pray to You and keep my ever-present faith and trust in You God, to worship and praise you wherever I go, to keep my roots grounded in your firmness and rock-solid foundation, for I am waiting on you to answer my prayers in your GREAT timing, not mine. And until then, God, all I can do is trust what the scripture in Psalms 46:10 says, "Be still and know that I'm God." God, I present and ask these requests in the name of Jesus…Amen.

~Brian Pinson

Help Is On The Way

2 Chronicles 20:15

And he said, "Pay attention all Judah, and those dwelling in Jerusalem, and King Jehoshaphat: Thus says the Lord to you, 'Do not fear, nor be dismayed because of this great army, for the battle is not 'yours, but God's.

Lord Jesus, we thank you for being the Prince of Peace and our Savior! We declare that this is our day of turnaround! Lord, you see the battles we are fighting, Lord we feel submerged and overwhelmed by life's battles! Lord, you are sovereign, and NOTHING catches you by surprise! First Lord, we thank you that you are teaching us how to fight our battles without ARMOR and without our natural strength or ability! But God that you are teaching us how to fight in the spirit, that you Lord are strengthening our spirit man even now! We thank you that your word declares that we should cast our cares upon you because YOU CARE! We thank you, Lord, that what that means to us is that HELP is ON THE WAY! WE stand in expectation of giving all our fears, doubts, worries, cares, and problems over to your mighty capable redeeming hand! Lord! If we don't SEE it happen today, we will get up tomorrow, declaring it to be a day of turnaround!

We believe you are working it out in our favor God! Lord, you did not give us the spirit of fear, but of Love power and of a sound mind, we thank you, that we have no reason to fear because you are with us! Emmanuel! We thank you that you are ever near, a present help in the times of trouble, we can run to you! The name of the Lord is a strong tower, Lord we find safety in your name! We will continue to declare victory until our prayers are answered .according to your will Lord! You always cause us to triumph. We thank you that in and through you... WE WIN! We know you have a purpose in all things that you allow us to go through, and we will endure hardness as good soldiers. Our answer we will be YES, LORD! We won't back down. We won't be shaken by this! Whatever the "This" is right now, We won't be defeated in our chase of those things that you have already spoken about which belong to us. We will fight for our peace. We will fight for our renewed minds. We will fight discouragement and disappointment! We will fight negative thinking. We will fight doubt, we will fight! And we WILL win! This day, Lord, we speak life! Will we no longer speak words, but we will speak FAITH! We will confuse the enemy and speak well in troubled times. We will have a praise on our lips and Joy in our hearts! We will not allow the enemy to stifle our praise or worship, which is due you, Father! We declare In Jesus' Name, that the battle is NOT ours, but it is the Lords. We thank you for the expiration date you have placed on our troubles, and we place our hope in you, in the name Jesus, Amen!

~Renee Myers

Jesus, Save Me

Lord God,

I am not good at this, and I really don't know how to pray, but I need your help. I am broken, and I am ashamed. I have been hurt, and I have hurt others. My life is filled with pain. Someone told me that you love me with an everlasting love, so much so that Jesus gave his life for me so that I would not have to pay the penalty of death for my sins. Your son, who committed no sin, died so that I can live again. They said you are a very present help in trouble. I was told that if I call on the name of Jesus, I will be saved. They said you could heal my broken heart, deliver me from my fears and all my destructive ways. They said you would teach me what I must do to be saved. So, here I am, God, laying myself before you. A broken and contrite heart they said you would not despise. Please hear from me, Lord. I am so tired. Please, forgive me of all my sins.

Teach me your ways so that I can follow. I was told that Jesus came so that I could have life and that more abundantly. I pray to experience the abundant life. They told me about your kingdom, and in your kingdom, there is peace and there is joy. They said there is a joy that gives strength to the weak. I pray to experience the peace and the joy of the Lord. And I thank you that where I am weak, you will make me strong. I know you have so much more for me. Open the eyes of my understanding to the truth and the knowledge of you so that I may have the abundant life and be all that you purposed me to be. In Jesus name I pray. Amen

~Mya Jackson Brown

Defeating Self-Doubt

PSALMS: 34:4

I sought the Lord, and he answered me, and delivered me from all my fears.

When I look in the mirror, I see a shell of a woman that was admired and accepted by others. The deeper I stare, the less I see. Who am I? What happened to her? Why do I doubt myself? What am I afraid of?

Heavenly Father, I come to you unsure, uneasy, and doubtful. God, I ask you to make me whole to give me the strength to believe in myself. I have spent too many years relying on the approval of others. Today, I ask for your approval, your strength, and your direction. God, I need you like never before. I ask you to give me your eyes so that I can see the reflection in the mirror. I ask you to speak to my heart, reminding me that you are here today, yesterday, and tomorrow. I ask you to speak to the doubts that flood my mind at night and stall my movements during the day. I ask that you give me the strength to give all my negative thoughts to you. I ask that you help silence the *enemy* when he speaks untruthful things about me. I ask that these things no longer clutter my mind or dim my spirit. God, I ask you to remind me to slow down and breathe during those times when I cannot move or decide. I ask all these things in your son Jesus' name. AMEN.

~Toni G. Guy

Sustain Me with Your Grace

Lord, I come to you broken-hearted, confused, and unsure what to do in this situation. You are my refuge, my only hope, the only place I know to turn. The enemy is trying to take me out. This is a blind-sided attack that reaches great depths. I am weak, and I am tired. How long must I endure this agony?

All I can do is Trust in You and your Word... You said
Let the weak say I'm strong, so I say, *I'm strong!*
You said to fear not, so *I will not fear!*
You said not to lean toward my own understanding of things
So I'm desperately trying to keep my eyes fixed on you, your love, your grace, your power.

Sustain me with your Grace O God.
Blind my eyes to my problem and guide me through this temporary circumstance.
Envelope me with the strength to endure.
Allow my mind to rest knowing that you have this entire situation in your hands and under your control. I trust you, and I'm nothing without you. Hear my prayer, oh Lord.

In Jesus Name I pray. Amen.

~Cynthia Knight

Cast Your Cares On God

1 Peter 5:7

"Cast all your anxiety on him because he cares for you."

Dear Lord,

When my heart is heavy, when I am hurting, and when I have fallen short of where I desire to be in life: lift up my head, renew my mind and help me to see the truth through You. Hardships and disappointments are all around me. When I feel nervous, restless, and all alone; still, I have hope in You. I lay every burden at Your feet. Fill me up, oh Lord, because I am running low on patience. Calm my anxious spirit and pour Your hope and steadfastness in me. When I am crushed by fears and worry consumes me, remind me of Your grace and power. I desire more of You, God. Draw me closer to You. Give me the joy that surpasses all understanding. You dry the weeping tears from my eyes and free my heart from turmoil. I will look to the hills from which comes my help because I know that my help comes from the Lord! Let me not be anxious for anything, but in everything, by prayer and petition, with thanksgiving, I make my request to You, God. Fill me with Your peace as I trust in You and You alone. Show me that everything works according to Your righteous plan, and please take care of the smallest details. Thank You for restoring my joy, hope and faith. My faith will cast out all of my fears. You get all of the glory. Hallelujah is the highest praise that I can give.

~Minister Mishawn A. Jones

Lord, I Need You!

Lord, today I want you to know how much I am grateful that you are in My life. Lord, I need you in every area of my life. There are circumstances and situations that I cannot properly articulate; however, you seem to know when to step in on my behalf.

I am so grateful that you are in my life. When I think about the times that you have covered me, protected me, fought for me, provided for me, healed me, and come through on my behalf, I am overwhelmed with gratitude. As I face current life challenges, the old song comes to mind. "I need thee O Lord, every hour, I come to thee." I come to you, Lord, because I know that I can trust you. I have a track record with you. I have history with you. And you have never ever left me. God, I thank you for your very presence. I appreciate your mere presence in my life. You are not just hovering over me, but you are an active and present force in my life. Thank you, Jesus!

I know that you promised that you would never leave nor forsake me. I invite you into every area of my life. God be with me in my home. Be with me at work. I need your presence in my business. I need you when I am driving or on public transportation.

Father, I need you to bless the work of my hands. In fact, I know that it is you who gives me the power to get wealth, so I ask you, kind father, to anoint and bless me with the ability to develop multiple streams of income. I ask you to turn my talents into resources. God turn my talents and hobbies into enterprises and businesses. Multiply my creativity. Give me new and innovative ideas, instructions, and insight.

Lord, I give my talents back to you. Help me not to bury or squander them, but rather use them for the upbuilding of your kingdom. I ask you to enable me to use every gift, every skill and every talent to edify and uplift others.

Lord, I want to walk worthy of being your child. I ask you to lead and guide me closer to my destiny. If you lead me, then I cannot go astray. I want to walk in ordered steps, Lord. As I do so, I ask that you reveal your purpose to me. As you do, I ask you to equip me to fulfill it.

Finally, Lord, I know that seasons and people change. Therefore, I ask you to guide me through the changing seasons in my life. Lead me as relationships shift. I am mindful that you, God, are the constant in my life. I am thankful that you promised never to leave nor forsake me. As other things shift in my life, I pray that I be ever mindful of your stabilizing presence. As it has previously made a difference in my life, it will continue to do so. I thank you, Lord, for meeting me at the point of my needs, in Jesus' name Amen!

~Evangelist Teraleen R. Campbell

MUSTARD SEED FAITH

Dear Heavenly Father,

Thank you! Thank you for your grace and mercy. Lord, thank you for keeping me. Heavenly Father, I come as I am lacking faith. I come to you asking for my faith to be restored. Hebrews 11:1 states, "Faith is the substance of things hoped for, the evidence of things not seen." I pray that you provide me with the substance of things hoped for. Lord, I know that having faith will see me through every trial, but sometimes it is a challenge for me to spiritually see. I do not trust myself when making certain decisions pertaining to my life. I am asking for the spiritual vision needed to make decisions that align with you, God. Heavenly Father, guide me to make sound choices through faith and hope. Thank you, Lord, for keeping me. I ask these things in Your son's Jesus Christ's name, Amen.

~LaShaviar S. Burns

GRIEF, LOSS, and BROKEN HEARTED

For the Broken Hearted

Dear Lord,

Your word says, "You will never leave me nor forsake me," but there are often times I feel sad, lonely, vulnerable and unsure of your presence. Even as I grieve, carry me, give me peace and comfort knowing that You sent Your Holy Spirit to hold me, even during times, I may not always feel You near. Give me the understanding and peace to let go and let God. Give me the patience to let time heal my wounds and the Creator to restore my soul. My solemn prayer is that you restore unto me the joy of my salvation so that my heart and mind are fixed on You as You do Your perfect work within me. Cover my family and friends, especially those who suffer in silence...remind them that they are never alone. Continue to be a friend to the friendless, a father to the fatherless, and a mother to the motherless. Remind us that You catch every tear that falls from our eye and that you are a God that heals, restores, and renews. Strengthen our faith and let us know that You are God and that You do all things well. Let us not lean on our own understanding but trust the plans that You have for us. Give us the patience, courage, and peace to move on day by day, knowing that our times and seasons are in Your hands. Grant us safety and assurance, knowing that we are Your children, and You love us unconditionally and wholeheartedly.

~Dr. Toyia K. Younger

DEALING WITH UNEXPECTED LOSS

Introduction:

My family recently experienced the loss of two family members in less than a month. Both unexpected and both brother and sister. This was a time the family really had to trust God to help us through this hour of loss.

Prayer:

Most Sovereign God. You are the One that comforts beyond human understanding. The experience of loss during this hour has been tremendous, but you are the one that can give strength and peace amid a broken heart riddled with grief. You are our strength during times of loss.

There may be times it's hard to accept your will, but we trust you. We pray that you continue to wrap your arms around those that have had to say goodbye to loved ones. Allow them to know that You are the God of peace, The God of all comfort. And even in this, You are still God.

The God that mends the broken hearted. You can heal what You create. You see us in this. There is no sorrow that You do not know about. Your promise is You would never leave us nor forsake us. You know what we are facing, and You are in it with us.

Cover our homes, cover our emotions, cover our hearts. We believe you will continue to be the strength like no other. Thank You, we pray and believe, Amen.

~Reverend Darryl D. Brookins

Heal My Heart Lord

Psalm 34:18

The Lord is close to the brokenhearted and saves those who are crushed in spirit.

Lord, it's me again. I come to your throne of grace, asking you first to forgive me for all of my sins, asking that you would hear my petition before you, Lord, that you Jesus would intercede on my behalf as I pray this prayer today! Lord, I am here before you in a hurt/ broken state. God, I feel so alone right now…When I open my mouth, anger, bitterness or strife comes out instead of your love, instead of your word and patience!

Lord, I am walking around with a spirit of offense. I am walking and operating in a broken space. Lord, I desire to meet you halfway and lay it all down at your feet right NOW! You told me in your word Lord, to cast my cares before you because you care for me. You care about my cries. You care about my hurt, you care about my pain, about my discouragements, Father, I know you care for me. I am your child! Lord, thank you for saving my soul, thank you for the blood of Jesus you left for me to use as an authority and weapon by faith! Please heal my heart Lord. Breathe new life within me! My heart needs to be repaired from the spirit of offense and hurt! Even in my crushed state, Lord, I STILL desire to please you. Lord, I want you to get the Glory out of my life! Thank you for walking close to me and not leaving me in the state of my pain. I desire to walk in the truths that your word has provided unto me that makes me free! Free my crushed spirit. Make me a new creation in you, Lord! I understand God that prayer is the place burdens change shoulders! Thank you that your shoulders can bear my burdens and FIGHT all my battles! Thank you for giving us a heart of flesh again and taking away the one I allowed to be stone. Thank you for a heart that is tender again, that is able to love and believe again! Thank you, Lord, for a new spirit, and I BELIEVE it is done in the name Jesus!

Amen

~Renee Myers

S(he) Cries in the Dark

Matthew 11:28-30; Psalm 6; Ps 9:9; Ps 46:1, I0; Psalm 56:8-9; Isaiah 55:11; Jeremiah 31:3; John 10:10; Romans 8:15; 2; Timothy 1:7; I Peter 1:8-9, 5:7; Hebrews 13:5; I John 4:18.

Come unto Me, you who are weary and carry a heavy burden. Come to Me and I will give You rest, a true refreshing for Your life. I AM a refuge for the oppressed, a refuge and strength, a very present help in times of trouble. I have heard Your pleadings. I immediately turned to listen when You cried unto me, "LORD HELP! Don't You hear my groanings and how I cry out to You?!" My child, I have taken hold of Your prayers and answered them ALL because I care for You.

Lift up Your head. There is no need for You to hide Your face from Me. I AM gentle, humble, and easy to please. All that I require of You will be pleasant and easy to bear. COME! Cast all Your cares, anxieties, worries, and concerns upon Me. Allow *Me* to wipe away the tears You cry in the dark. Yes, I see Your tears. I see them before they form. I can taste the saltiness before they fall. I AM *El Roi,* the Mighty God who sees. I--*SEE--YOU.* So, *come.* I do not wish to enslave but loose You from Your bondages and set You free in Your innermost being, in Your soul (mind, will, emotions). Neither torment, nor indecision, nor fear should be Your bread. I AM Your Daily Bread, and I have come to feed You, strengthen You, and give You life in abundance; love, power, and soundness of mind are Your inheritance.

So come, come out of the darkness into My marvelous light. In My Light, darkness cannot hide and it *cannot* hide You. I AM Your hiding place. Your place of shelter. Come. Tuck Yourself in the crevice of My shadow-in My secret place-and I will show You the paths of life. In My presence is fullness of joy. At My right hand, there are pleasures forever more. Come, seek Me and You will find Me---{t)here--drawing You with My loving kindness. Guiding, leading directing, pulling You out of *Your* hiding place. There is no need to fear. Perfect love, My agape love, drives out all fear. Trust Me.

I have not left You, nor have I forsaken You. I AM a keeper of My Word. I AM *THAT I* AM. My Word cannot return unto Me void. You cannot be (a) voided! Before the beginning of chronos, I was (t)here. You are always in My thoughts... {t)here, then, now, forever Kairos. Even in this place of *Your* temporary shelter, You are *not* alone. You were *never* alone. You were *never* orphaned. You have been adopted by the Most-High God! You are Mine-a royal priesthood-and I AM Your ABBA Father. Yes, You are peculiar because You have been grafted into *My* bloodline. You are privileged to COME! Do not be ashamed of Your tears. I bottle every one of them, for they are precious to ME. COME, bring them to me, and I will give You rest for Your soul!

~Elder Alicia A. Richardson

God's Abiding Comfort

Hebrews 4:15; Psalms 147:3; Philippians 4:6; John 14:1, 27;
Psalms 56:8; Philippians 4:7

Matthew 5:4; Psalm 34:18; I Thessalonians 4:13

Father, I thank you that we have a High Priest Who is able to understand and sympathize with our weakness. Father, hear my prayer and grant me peace that passes all understanding. Show me the way to Your throne that I may sit at your feet and know Your abiding comfort. Let a wellspring of joy rise from my heart until it overflows. Father, remove my anger and replace it with a great acceptance of Your will. I pray for healing of my sadness and constant grief.

Father, my heart is broken, my mind exhausted. As I cry out to You, keep track of my sorrows and collect all my tears in Your bottle. Father, I'm mourning, so I ask for Your comfort. Shower Your comfort on me through those around me. Show me new ways to cope with my loss that will renew my mind and refill my heart with Your eternal love. Take the consuming anguish I feel right now; take it from me and hold me in Your arms. Heal my broken heart and bind up my wounds.

Father, Your word says, "Do not let your hearts be troubled. You believe in God; believe in Me. It also says, "Peace I leave with you; My peace I give you. I do not give to you as the world gives." I need Your peace. I need "the peace of God, which transcends all understanding" to guard my heart and mind. I need peaceful sleep. I ask for peaceful thoughts and emotions to rule my days and nights.

Father, I thank You that You are "close to the brokenhearted and [You rescue] those whose spirits are crushed." Draw close to me and rescue me. Help me not to grieve like those who haven't discovered Your kindness and mercy, who have no hope; lift me up and give me hope once more. Help me to believe that tomorrow will be better, and the next day will be easier and that a day will come when I will feel a surge of energy and expectation for what You are doing and where You will take me.

Father, thank you for giving me beauty for ashes, the oil of joy for mourning, the garment of praise for the spirit of heaviness. Your word is my hope. It revives me and comforts me. Thank you for being Immanuel,

God with me. In the name of Jesus I pray, amen.

God's Promise for healing the Broken Hearted

Come to me, all you who are weary and burdened, and I will give you rest. Take my yoke upon you and learn from me, for I am gentle and humble in heart, and you will find rest for your souls. For my yoke is easy and my burden is light. Matthew 1 1:28-30

So with you: Now is your time of grief. but I will see you again and you will rejoice, and no one will take away your joy. John 1 6:22

~Bridgette L. Threat

A Long Night

Dear Heavenly Father,

How are you? I am believing awesome. Lord, allow me to thank you for your ever-present in my life even when I do not acknowledge you. It is because of Your grace and mercy that I am able to see a brand-new day. With this new day, Lord, I ask that you search me and know my heart. Heavenly Father, I ask you to come into my heart and free me from the bitterness I am holding on to that brings no joy. Lord, my heart aches, but I am trusting you to restore it. I know you are a healer and a restorer because Psalms 139: 1 states, "O Lord, you have examined my heart and know everything about me." With this verse alone, you know my heart hurts. You know my mind follows my heart. Lord, {transparency moment} "I'm tired and don't see any relief of this pain in sight because it has been years. God, I trust you because weeping may endure for a night, but joy comes in the morning (Psalms 30:5). Heavenly Father, it has been a long night, and you do your best work at night. Lord, I ask that you continue working on my heart during the night so I may see joy when I wake up. Thank you, Lord, in Jesus' name, Amen.

~LaShaviar S. Burns

A Heart of Sorrows

PSALMS 34:18

The Lord is close to the brokenhearted and saves those who are crushed in spirit.

Heavenly Father, my heart is broken into a million pieces. Every ounce of my being was devoted to loving them, and yet they still decided to leave. I postponed dreams, sacrificed myself, and even shut you out because I loved them. I keep asking myself, why wasn't I enough? Why wasn't my love?

This weight is unbearable, and I don't know how I will be able to go on. God, I beg you to take this pain away. You promised that you would never leave nor forsake me, and I need to know that you are still here. I know that there is no love like yours, and I am asking for just a piece of it, even if I don't deserve it. God, I ask one day that you can heal me and make me strong again. I want to smile again, laugh again, and love again. This time I need you to show me how to do all these things YOUR WAY. God, I ask for forgiveness for abandoning you and putting the selfish love ahead of your selfless love. Please forgive me and mend my broken heart. AMEN.

~Toni G. Guy

Lord, Avenge Me

Father, we are coming crawling to you on our knees. They left; they left us all alone. We have never been alone, Lord. They said goodbye and walked out of our lives. We are trying to be strong, but it hurts too much. What will we do? what should we say? What about the years we spent together? What about the vows we took for better or worse? Crying so much, we can barely see. We think we are dying; this must be death; we cannot feel anything but pain. Lord, they do not love us anymore.

Ok Lord, now we are angry. How can they do this to us? They promised to love us forever. How dare they leave us. Who do they think they are? Ok, Lord, now we are ready to fight back. Let us hurt them like they hurt us. Great, yes, it's time for battle. Ahh, Lord, we do not hear you saying let us go.

Lord, your word says Isaiah 54: 17, "No weapon formed against us shall prosper," so let's go get them, right? They can get away with this. We are children of the Almighty God. In Deuteronomy 31:6, You said, "Be strong and courageous. Do not be afraid or terrified because of them, for the LORD your God with us; you would never leave or forsake us". Look, God, we need to strike back, like right now. We do not like feeling pain. It is too much, Lord. Please take it away.

Lord, what is this, you say. Stand still?? How can we get them by standing still? It's time to get them back, Lord. Stop playing. Huh, what is this you want us to read in your word? Exodus 14: 14 reads, The Lord will fight for us; we only need to be still.

Ok, we get it, Lord. But doing nothing and being still is now making us feel angry. How can we deal with these raw feelings of anger? We feel like we need to lash out before we explode. Ok, Lord, we will continue reading. James 1:19 "My dear sisters, take note of this: Everyone should be quick to listen, slow to speak, slow to become angry. We hear you, Lord; we are starting to calm down now. Thank you.

So, Lord, are you saying that we need to change, not them? We want to be different, but we do not know how to change. We want to feel better, but how? Romans 12 "Bless those who persecute us, bless and do not curse. Do not repay anyone evil for evil. Do not take revenge, my dear friend, but leave room for God's wrath. Well, alright then, we like where this is going.

Ok, we get it. Not our way but your way. We will follow your lead. We will wait on you. We will pray to you for guidance. Thank you for saving us from ourselves. We cannot do anything without you. We really need you. Thank you for continuing to bless us even when we do not deserve it. Thank you for stopping us. Thank you for loving us. Peter 3:9 "Don't repay evil with evil or insult with insult. Repay evil with blessings because you all were called to inherit a blessing.

Lord, thank you for stepping in and reminding us of your promises, your word, and your love. We feel better now. Philippians 4:6-7 "Be anxious about anything, but in every situation, by prayer and petition, with thanksgiving, present your requests to God, which transcends all understanding. I will guard your heart and your mind in Christ Jesus. AMEN.

~Terry Wedlock

Beauty for Ashes

Blessed are those who mourn, for they will be comforted.
Matthew 5:4

God, I thank you for being the God of comfort and for your word that reminds me that you are close to the broken hearted and will bind up our wounds. Lord, a grieving heart is a broken heart, and the despair can run deep. Your Word tells me to let not my heart be troubled, and I am grateful that you have all the pieces of my broken heart in your hands. When I feel that I may never stop crying, you understand each and every one of my tears. You have held me close and rocked me in your bosom when I felt lost and all alone. In the times that I have felt out of control, you calmed my spirit, and you gave me rest. Lord, comfort those who are grieving today. There are so many people who are hurting and so many things that are breaking our hearts. Father, if it's Covid or any other dreadful diseases, please be Jehovah Rapha. If it's missing a loved one, allow the Holy Spirit to bring Comfort. If there is a loss of income, loss of employment, the loss of a home or a vehicle or a lifestyle, please be Jehovah Jireh and be the great Provider. Lord, your word says that you will comfort all who mourn and provide for all those who grieve. Restore our hearts to joy and gladness. Give us our crown of beauty and remove these ashes. Father, we are ready for our garment of praise instead of this spirit of despair (Isaiah 61:3). Father, please be the heart fixer that is needed where your people are mourning and allow us the benefit of peace. Send your healing, Lord. Little by little, allow your light to take over the darkness that has taken over. Bring back the hope and the zeal for life that once was. Lord, please hear my prayer. It is in the Name above all other Names that I pray. And I say, Amen!

~Minister Michelle Lee

Even If You Don't

Daniel 3:17-18, Psalms 33:20, 46:1

*Excerpt from «Letter to God», Lyrics by Jaye Harmon
and prayer by Minister A. Lynae Brooks*

Dear God, here I am torn and just a bit confused,
Cause I know with You, there's just no way that I'll ever lose.
Yet this pain I feel so great,
and it appears You hesitate to bring me out. So,
now I call to You,
please hear my plea. My
life belongs to You· come
see about me.
But even if You don't I understand, and I
know that You still can.

Dear God, please tell me everything will be OK,
that You've heard my cry and angels You'll send right away. And
they'll come to rescue me,
and in exchange for all this pain, they'll give me peace. So,
with my broken heart
I cry to You
cradle me in Your arms
as only You can do,
But even if You don't, I'll understand,
and I know that still, You can

Dear God, today, my heart lifts up those who are battling great pain, great loss, uncertainty, and unbearable situations. I come before You now crying out on behalf of every wounded heart. I ask that You saturate everyone with an "even if You don't" stance. Too often in life, we see so much, we experience so much, we endure severe trials, challenges, and adversities; and at the very end of it all, we look to You for help. Jehovah Ezer, You are the Lord of my help; a very present help in the time of trouble. I turn to You not for what You can do, but because of who You are. I know in the mighty name of Jesus that You are able to do anything but fail. That there is nothing impossible for You, and we put our complete and total trust in You.

I speak right now and in the name of Jesus to the spirit of disappointment, the spirit of frustration, the spirit of defeat, and the spirit that is ready to give up before the blessing arrives. God, I pray in the name of Jesus that You clothe them with a garment that drapes them with a "I'm not letting You go till you bless me" attitude! That they may stand flat footed in who You are and not what You do! You are I AM, that I said I AM! I speak in the name of Jesus, let the "even if You don't" spirit ignite! If the business doesn't take off the way I expect, I understand. If the chemo doesn't cure the cancer, I understand. If I lose the house and have to start over again, I understand. If the relationship never mends, I understand. If I lose the baby I've waited all my life for, I understand! If I have to serve even longer, and I never get the recognition, I understand. If I have to stay single even longer, I understand. If the trials and adversities keep coming like a raging storm, I understand. And no matter what happens I know You can! No matter what I see, I know You can! No matter what I feel, I know You can! On Your word that never fails, I know You can! Even if You don't, I understand and I know that You still can! Lord, I praise You, I honor You, and I exalt Your name above every name! No matter how the situation or circumstances that I encounter turn out, I trust You. I believe in You and I put my hope in You. I relinquish the complete and total resolve of my understanding in You! Raise my measure of faith, raise my understanding in You! In the name of Jesus, I decree and declare that it is so!

~Minister A. Lynae Brooks

Through it All - Thank You!

Grief is not just the loss or the death of a loved one. Grief can also include the loss of friendships and other relationships. It can involve losing a job, losing a home and yes, physical death. Simply put, grief is the natural reaction to disruption or loss.

As we consider the various people and things that we have lost, a sense of sadness inevitably comes over us. I for one have recently experienced loss of employment due to downsizing, and loss of family members, in addition to the loss of my doggie.

Navigating through life in unchartered territory brings a myriad of emotions, BUT God is with us. We can be rest assured that the Lord remains with us through all the changes within our lives. That promise alone should give us a dose of comfort and encouragement.

The Lord promised that he would be with us in Isaiah 41:9-10.

For I have chosen you
and will not throw you away.
Don't be afraid, for I am with you.
Don't be discouraged, for I am your God.
I will strengthen you and help you.
I will hold you up with my victorious right hand.

During those times when our hearts feel overwhelmed, we can go to Jesus, who is our rock. The beauty is that He too is acquainted with grief and has carried our sorrows. In other words, He knows, He hears, and He will help us!

Prayer

Lord, I admit that the losses I have encountered have left me feeling sad and have put me into a low place. I am now realizing that it wasn't just the deaths but the losses that keep mounting, and they have made me weary. Alas, I realize I can be open and honest with you regarding where I am. I wouldn't have wanted to lose the people or things, but I bow to your ultimate will, as painful as it is.

God, there are days when I don't want to get out of bed. There are days when I want to pull the covers over my head and sleep through it all. There are days when I feel only heaviness. Then I remember that you are the ultimate lifter, and I muster up the strength to get up and even to rejoice. You give me reason to rejoice!

I thank you, Lord, for being a promise-keeping God. I know that it is you who has been keeping me on my feet. You have kept me going. Through it all, you have not left me. I pray in Jesus' name that you remove the darkness that seeks to hover over me. I decree and declare that I will not live or walk in darkness, for it is not your will. Although I grieve that which is gone, I will not get stuck in grief. Lord, help me to walk in the newness of this life. Let the sunshine again in my life. Smile on me, Lord!

I thank you and ask that you strengthen me, give me wisdom and peace as I continue on this next leg of my life's journey. I cannot make it without you. I thank you for the assurance that just as you have been with me to this point, you will remain. I thank you for your presence. It is literally giving me life.

This is my prayer today, in Jesus' name. Amen

~Evangelist Teraleen R. Campbell

DELIVERANCE

THE GOD WHO SEES ME

Jehovah Gibbor, we come to you just to say thank you. You are a mighty God. Lord, you are mighty in battle, and you are our banner. We look to you, O God, because you have already won the battle. Your words say that victory belongs to You. We trust in you because you have never failed us. Jehovah Gibbor, God, you are mighty and mighty in battle. God, you are a strong tower and a deliverer; we praise and magnify your name. You are the God-of the valley and a God of the mountains. Your word shall not come back void but should accomplish everything that you decreed and declared it to do. Lord, send your Heavenly Army of angels to deliver me. The enemy is attacking me, but I know that you will fight for me, Jehovah Gibbor. Come to my aid and rescue me from my enemies. God fulfill Your work in my life and give me relief from those who want to kill and destroy me. The enemy opposes Your word, truth, and light, but let your justice prevail in my life. Come Lord Jesus and deliver your servants. Surround us with Your strength and shield. You alone are God. Jehovah Sabaoth, the Lord of Host, I need you. Lord, I pray that in this life, when the things of the world surround us and try to pull us away, that You would come to our aid like you did for David , when the bear attacked his sheep. You're the great Shepherd that protects your people. Lord, lead us beside still waters and take our burdens and give us rest. I pray that through the valley, You would lead us to safety. You are our Father, leader, and protector. Lead us in Your truth, for Your glory. Just as Hagar wept in the desert for want of life-giving nourishment, I pray that You would be the God Who Sees Me! El Roi, come to our rescue! You are not a God far off, but one that is near. You are a good Shepherd that never leaves His flock alone. I pray that when my circumstances pile up on me that you would see my needs and attend to my burdens. Lord, I am surrounded by my problems, but you are my help and strength. I pray that You would be my strength and that You would come and surround me as the mountains surround Jerusalem. I pray that You would be El Shaddai to me, the One Who Is Sufficient for me. Though we may be poor, weary and have nothing in this life, I can be content because I have You. El Roi, nothing can escape You. Come to deliver me when I am in trouble. It is the anointing that breaks every yoke, all generational curses over my life, home and family and chains and shackles. Deliver us from the antichrist, limitation, and curses. In Jesus Name, Amen.

~Minister Melissa Powell-Harrell

Free-ish

John 8:36, Philippians 4:7

Most gracious and eternal Father I come before You petitioning for those individuals who are free in their body but not in their mind. God, so often we find happiness in our lives, yet our minds are bombarded with stress, problems, to-do lists, inadequacies, turmoil, phobias, being overwhelmed, full of fear, and the list goes on and on. I come before You casting down every vain imagination that rises itself up against Your great and mighty spirit. You said in Your word, who the son sets free is free indeed! I speak to the bodies that are free and minds that are being held in captivity, You shall no longer be free-ish. I bind the spirits of confusion, turmoil, mental illness, anguish, overwhelming, delusions, perversion, illicit imaginations, anxieties, depression, anger, destructive thoughts, suicide, and every contrary thought in hidden places of the mind in the name of Jesus. I loose the spirit of Your perfect peace to permeate the mind in every bound place that is now empty.

I praise You right now for the immediate manifestation of Your peace. You, said in Isaiah 26:3, "You will keep him in perfect peace, whose mind is stayed on You because he trusts in You." I trust You! I know You and I pray for every opportunity that the enemy attempts to infiltrate Your peace within the minds of Your people. Even now, I come against every plot and plan of the enemy to place Your precious people back in the state of free-ish and I speak to every area that is bound and command it in Jesus' name to remain free! As 2 Corinthians 10:5 teaches us, "we demolish arguments and every pretension that sets itself up against the knowledge of God, and we take captive every thought to make it obedient to Christ." I speak complete and total freedom, free in the mind, free in the body, and free in the spirit. Be free and walk in the fullness of all that God has called and purposed You to be, in the mighty name of Jesus I pray. This is Your season of freedom! Amen

~Minister A. Lynae Brooks

Deliverance from Defeating Thoughts

Father, we thank you that you are a good father and that you desire to see your children live free from fear, impotence, and ignorance. Your word declares in 2 Timothy 1:7 You did not give us the spirit of fear but instead gave us love, power, and a sound mind. You also told us in Isaiah 55:8 and 9, your thoughts are not ours and your ways high above ours, therefore we wage a battle against our defeating thoughts. Our thoughts have caused us to live in ways contrary to the authority you gave us to speak things and they become established according to Job 22:28.

We ask that you deliver us from low-level thoughts which cause low levels of action. We renounce all manner of self-defeating thoughts and paradigms which cause us to demonstrate actions inconsistent with your purpose for our lives. We desire to have manifestations of your glory be revealed in our lives through seeing momentum activated and stagnation destroyed. We declare that we have Your mind in operation in our daily activities, and others will come to know You in a more excellent way because of our transformation. We will be delivered from fear and anxiety through your love motivating us to live, move, and have our being according to Acts 17:28. We will no longer trust the lies the enemy tells us about ourselves, causing us to amplify our failures over our successes. We say to the enemy of defeat - we have everything we need that pertains to our life and Godliness.

We will not be moved from our convictions. We will declare your word that tells us in Romans 8:31, "If God be for us, who can be against us?" We will walk in the liberty wherein You have set us free, and we will not be entangled with yokes of bondage that cause us to regress. Our hope will be found in You, and we will prevail over the schemes of our adversary who has come to steal our joy, peace, and livelihood. We will trust in You who has come to give us an abundant life according to John 10:10. We praise you because you have carefully crafted us in your image and likeness. We believe that because your breath is in us you will always cause us to triumph even when we feel like we are losing the battle. God, we thank you because you NEVER MISS a target and with your direction leading us, we will WIN! Amen.

~Terralyn Frazier

Deliver Me

Hebrews 4:16; 1 John 5:14; Matthew 18:18; James 4:7; Psalms 107:2; Luke 10:19; Colossians 1:13; Hebrews 12:1

Father, I come boldly to the throne of grace to find help, strength, and deliverance in my time of need. Father, You said that if I ask anything according to Your will, You would hear and answer me. Father, I know it is Your will for me to be delivered and walk in deliverance therefore, I ask that You deliver me from _____

Father, You said that whatever I bind on earth is bound in heaven, and whatever I loose on earth is loosed in heaven. You said for me to cast out demons in the name of Jesus. I bind my mind, will and emotions to the will and purposes of God for my life. I bind my mind to the mind of Christ that every thought, feeling and purpose of His heart would be within my thoughts.

I loose every old, ungodly, wrong pattern of thinking, attitude, desire, habit and behavior from my life. I tear, crush and destroy every stronghold associated with things in my life that are not like You. I loose any stronghold in my life that I might be justifying. I say Satan shall not get any advantage over my life, for I am not ignorant of Satan's devices. I resist Satan, and he must flee in the name of Jesus. I give Satan no place in my life. I thank You Father, that I am redeemed out of the hand of Satan by the blood of Jesus.

I thank You Father, that I tread on serpents and scorpions and over all the power of the enemy. I declare I am delivered from this present evil world. I declare I am delivered from the powers of darkness and translated into the Kingdom of Your dear Son. Father, I stand firm in my place of victory whereby You have set me free. I refuse to be further entangled with the yoke of bondage, I lay aside every weight and sin which would hold me back, and I run with patience, the race that is set before me.

I thank You Father, that Jesus was manifested that He might destroy the works of the devil. Satan's works are destroyed in my life in the name of Jesus. I walk in the Kingdom of God, which is righteousness, peace, and joy in the Holy Spirit!

In the name of Jesus I pray, Amen.

God's Promise for Deliverance

The righteous cry out, and The Lord hears,

And delivers them out of all their troubles.

Psalms 34:1 7

Then they cried out to the Lord in their trouble,

And He delivered them out of their distresses.

Psalms 107:6

~Bridgette L. Threat

Don't Rush the Process

Proverbs 16:9, Jeremiah 29:11, Romans 8:28, Psalm 27:14

Father God, in the mighty name of Jesus, I come right now asking You to help me learn how to wait on You. There are things in my life that I desire to achieve and accomplish, but they just don't seem to come to pass. My desire is to please You above all. I know often I go my own way, or I try to make things happen within my power and might, and for that, I ask You to forgive me. You have given me the most precious gift of the Holy Spirit to lead me and guide me in all my ways, yet too often, I allow my voice, my immediate desire, family, and friends to veer me off my path or delay my progress. Forgive me, Lord! I know that Your promises are yes and amen, but Your timetable does match my expectations. Lord, help me to surrender my frustration, my agenda, my anticipations, my attitude and trust Your process. When I am uncertain, remind me that my steps are ordered by You. When I am impatient and ready to get further faster, please remind me that You know the plans that You have set for my life since the beginning of time. And most of all, when I hinder the process with procrastination, fear, impatience, rebellion, distractions, gently remind me to place my hope, my faith, and my trust in You for all things are working for my good. I know the process is not easy, for the race is not given to the swift or the battle to the strong but the one who endures to the end. Lord help me to endure! Help me to have unwavering confidence and a firm resolve that You know what's best for me. Help me to trust Your timing, Your delays, Your wait, Your no's, and Your pressure for me to pick up the pace and move faster. Incline my ear to hear You and my heart to obey. Holy Spirit, have Your way! Each day I pray, that You have free reign over the directions I will go. I pray in the mighty name of Jesus that I will forever enjoy the journey of "my process," learning and growing as I go! May I find You solace and comfort in the valleys, and may my praise echo on the climbs. When I reach the peaks, may I always look back and know that I could not make it without You. Hold my hand and lead me, and wherever You lead me Abba Father, I will go! In Jesus's name, I pray amen.

~Minister A. Lynae Brooks

SPIRITUAL WARFARE

We Advance In Battle

The Kingdom of God suffers violence and the violent take it by force!!! (Matthew 11:12)

God right now in the name of Jesus, I pray for the power of the Holy Spirit to fall in this prayer and the outcome of Victory to manifest.

I place on myself the full Armor of God to help me to stand against every scheme of the adversary according to Eph. 6:1 I call on Jehovah Gibbor to contend with everything that contends with me, according to Ps. 35:1, as I take territory against the kingdom of darkness in prayer.

I pray that the plans, plots, tools and tactics of the enemy be disintegrated now. Let everything the enemy thought he was going to use against me be dismantled. Every weapon being formed for my demise be rerouted back to its origin so that it does not prosper in accordance with Is. 54:17.

Every voice giving instructions against my purpose, destiny, children, family, growth, sanity, health, wholeness, wealth, abundance, and God purposed future, let it be fully consumed by the fire of the Holy Spirit now. Let it become ash and be blown away by the Ruach of God, in the name of Jesus.

I plead the Blood of Jesus against every hex, vex, incantation, enchantment, spell, lure, pull ungodly attraction sent my way to distract, retract, sidetrack, sideswipe, bewitch or bamboozle me. I declare and decree, a thousand may fall at my side and ten thousand at my right hand, but it will not come near me. I will only observe and see the destruction of the wicked, according to Psalm 91:7-8.

I rejoice, oh Lord, for you have given me victory over my enemies and put to shame those that hate me in accordance with Psalm 44:7, in Jesus' Mighty Name I pray. Amen

~Elder Elect Sonja Owens

Praying Against the Attack of the Enemy

It is no secret that the people of God are under attack. How do you know when you are on the enemy's hit list? When you are being hit after hit after hit. The hits come before you get the chance to recover. You also know when you begin to ask yourself what you have done to deserve this?

Take courage in knowing that it's not what you've done wrong, rather what you have done right. Your profession of faith in God has made you a threat to the enemy. He is sending his demons to come against you so that he can see if you are truly walking in and living what you have said. He wants you to give up. He wants to separate you from God.

This is where you must steady your shoulders and resolve not to back up, you should resolve not to back down. You cannot quit! You will not be defeated. 'According to the power that works in you.' You have to reach down inside of yourself and tap into the power of the Holy Spirit that resides on the inside of you. It is time to fight the enemy in prayer, going to battle for ourselves.

> *Now unto him that is able to do exceedingly abundantly above all that we ask or think, according to the power that worketh in us. Ephesians 3:20 KJV*

> *A final word: Be strong in the Lord and in his mighty power. Put on all of God's armor so that you will be able to stand firm against all strategies of the devil. Ephesians 6:10-11 NLT*

Prayer

Father, in the name of Jesus, Lord, you see the attacks, you see the weapons and darts that are being thrown at me. I need you to cover me. I ask you, Lord, to fight for me. I cannot win this battle without you.

I use the weapon of prayer at this moment to fight the attack of the enemy. I pray, kind father, in Jesus' name, that you bind every demonic attack. Lord, I plead the blood of Jesus over discouragement. Replace discouragement with holy boldness. You have not given us the spirit of fear, so God we decree and declare that we will not live-in fear, both in and outside of our homes. Cover our minds in the blood of Jesus. Do not allow us to be tormented in our minds due to our current situations.

Lord, I pray that you equip us for every battle that we are fighting. You said the weapons of our warfare are not carnal but mighty through you. With this in mind, we will not allow the devil's actions to prompt us to react in an ungodly manner that will bring reproach upon your name. You have given us the ability to pull down strongholds; therefore, we ask you to reveal them to us in the spirit and we will pull them down, in Jesus' name.

Many are they who rise against me. But thou O Lord are a shield for me. Finally, Father, we decree and declare that victory is imminent. We conclude this prayer by saying thanks be to God who giveth us the victory through our Lord Jesus Christ. Thank you for the victory! We see it before it comes and we thank you, in Jesus' name, Amen!

~Evangelist Teraleen R. Campbell

The Lord Mighty In Battle

Jehovah Gibbor, incline your ear to hear my prayer. Let my prayers reach the heavens and not be earth bound. Come and sit with me and hear my plea. God put your weight on me and fill me with your fire. Lord, you are my banner! When the enemy comes in like a flood, you allow me to stand and not be consumed. You alone give me victory in life. It is through Your Work on the Cross and the blood of Jesus Christ that gives me victory over the Evil One. Victory is mine because you are mighty in battle. When persecution comes, you are my refuge and fortress. Let me rest in your shadow. I can rest in the truth of Your Word. You are my Banner, as I go out into battle, I have strength because I serve You! Fortify me, Lord, as the things of this world surround me. Make me a fortified city or wall. Break the yoke of the enemy over my life. You Lord, rescue me, oh Lord, from my enemies and those who attempt to hinder, kill, and do harm to my life. The enemy comes to steal, kill and destroy, but you said you came that I might have life and have it more abundantly. My eyes are on you. You are my help. You are the God that helps your people. You will help and deliver me from all my enemies and the evil one. You deliver me from the fowlers snare and the deadly pestilence. You cover me with your feathers and under your wings. Build a shield around me. Lord, be a shield on my left, right, my front and back. It is your shield that protects and saves me. Fight the battle for me, Jehovah Gibbor. You have promised me victory. You, Lord, are righteous; you have cut me free from the cords of the wicked. I am weak, but you are strong. I will not fear the terror of night or the darts of the enemy because you are with me. I am nothing without you. You are with me. You are the God that protects me. You will not let me be consumed by the enemy and let harm overtake me. God, give me strength in my weakness. You will command your angels concerning me to protect and guide me from the evil one. You are the God of my salvation; I will trust in you and not be afraid. You are my strength and my defense and my salvation. In Jesus' Name, Amen.

~Minister Melissa Powell-Harrell

Weary In Warfare

Scripture references: 2 Chronicles 32:7-8;
Psalm 6: 55; Luke 22:31.

Father, in the name of Jesus, thank You for sending your ministering angels to your children who have become weary in the warfare. The devil desires to sift them as wheat, but I declare that their faith shall not fail because You Lord are their Intercessor. When they call, You will save! Evening, morning, and noon You hear their voice. I declare they shall not be oppressed by the wicked. You Lord will cause the enemy's deceit to depart from their midst. In times of trouble, have mercy upon them and deliver their soul in peace from the battles. You rescue your children without harm from the battles waged against them.

They shall not fear the spirit of death, nor be overwhelmed by the fiery darts because you are their Rock and their Shield. You will provide escape from the storms and shelter from the winds that beat upon them. You are a very present help!

Father, give them wings like a dove that they may fly above the calamity and be at rest. Cause them to be strong and courageous, not afraid nor dismayed of the multitude. Remind them that there are more with them than against and they can cast their burdens upon You. You shall sustain them, and You never allow the righteous to be moved. In Jesus's mighty name. AMEN and AMEN.

~ Elder Alicia A. Richardson

Power from On High

Father God, in the name of Jesus, we ask for your Holy Spirit to fill this place. You are the Holy Spirit that moved upon the deep. You are dumas. You are the giver of all revelation. We ask for you to anoint us from the top of our heads to the soles of our feet. Anoint us afresh so we look more like you and less like ourselves. We ask for you to anoint, overtake and empower us to do the work that you are calling us to do. Fill us like you did the apostles on the day of Pentecost.

We ask for fresh fire. Baptize us with your spirit of Fire. Empower us with your spirit to help us serve your people. We are asking for the impartation of your Holy Spirit. We ask that you anoint us afresh with the fire and power of the Holy Spirit. Let the fire fall in our lives, put your fire in our hands to heal the sick, the fire in our mouth to boldly declare your word; fire to preach and teach your word. Give us your fire to bring salvation to the unsaved. Give us the power that makes ministry easy; Give us the power that makes preaching easy. Give us the power, fortitude, and enduring spirit that makes ministry not a burden, task, but it is a pleasure, desire and want. You are a consuming fire. Consume us with the power of your Holy Spirit. We ask you to release us as your ambassadors on the earth, that we can walk boldly in the calling and anointing that you have given us. The power to break strongholds, overcome demonic enemies, and attacks. We ask that you anoint us afresh with your fire. Let your kabod fill this place. Let your weight, heaviness, and power fall on us. Come sit on us with your power. We speak to the atmosphere with your words which is life and power. We decree and declare that we walk in the authority and power you have given to your people. Let your fire destroy the enemy's plans and attempts to cause disunity, division, and chaos for your people. We will overcome the plans and plots of the enemy because we are filled with your power. We walk, talk, and operate in the power of your Holy Spirit.

In Jesus' Name, Amen.

~Minister Melissa Powell-Harrell

Set the Captives Free

"For though we walk in the flesh, we are not waging war according to the flesh. For the weapons of warfare are not of the flesh but have divine power to destroy strongholds. We destroy arguments and every lofty opinion raised against the knowledge of God and take every thought captive to obey Christ." - 2 Corinthians 10:3-5

God, we desperately seek your face today, calling on your name to break chains, destroy strongholds, and cast out demons, witches, and warlocks that are on the prowl for Your people. Wanting to keep them bound in their flesh and bound in their thoughts. We come up against any spirit that is not like you and we send it back to the pits of hell from whence it came. We come up against negativity in the name of Jesus. We come up against the spirit of descension that is running rampant throughout our city and state and through our families, turning son against father and mother against daughter. A house divided will not stand, so God, bind us all together with cords of love that cannot be broken.

Gird us up on every leaning side, that nothing can knock us down. Send Your angels to dispel the violence that is taking our youth and break the mental bondage that holds these parent's captive. Set them free God from their own way of thinking and thinking of others. Set them free from all the noise distractions of these TV shows and music on the radio. God, bring their children home never again to thirst for the things that are not like you. We cancel out every plan and trick of the enemy right now in the name of Jesus and we bring it under subjection of the Holy Spirit.

God, strengthen our faith and bring us to our knees so that we may hear you clearly and carry out Your will. God, I ask that you move throughout our educational systems, destroying policies that have been put in place to keep our children from receiving the education that is due them. God wipe out every witch that hides in the shadows and in plain sight, trying to control the things and people of God. We bind it up, and we loose the will of God. Have your way in, through, and around us. God, You said whatever we bind on earth shall be bound in heaven and whatever we lose on earth shall be loosed in heaven. So, we bind up malice and strife, greed and jealousy, pride and hatred and we loose love and compassion. We loose humility and generosity and we loose joy and peace. God, we believe you for all of this today. And we know that at the mention of Your name Jesus, demons tremble, at the mention of Your name Jesus, heaven responds, at the mention of Your name Jesus, every knee shall bow, and every tongue shall confess that Jesus Christ is Lord to the Glory of God the Father. Hallelujah and Amen!

~Minister Angelique M. Bullock

REVERSING GENERATIONAL CURSES

We praise you, oh Lord, for the redemptive power of the blood of Jesus Christ.

We thank you that according to Galatians 3:13-14, Christ hath redeemed us from the curse of the law being made a curse for us...that the blessing of Abraham might come upon us through Jesus Christ. For that reason, we reverse every demonic curse and release the blessing of Almighty God upon our lives.

We decree that our homes are blessed, our ministries are blessed, our businesses are blessed, and we are a source of blessing to others.

We pray that any claim that the enemy would use against us be removed and revoked. We decree by faith that his accusations will not stand in the courts of Heaven.

We enforce the proclamation that what the enemy would try to steal from us must be released, now.

As we approach the courts of Heaven, we take responsibility for the effect of generational sin in our family's bloodline.

We repent for the sins of our fathers. We repent and ask for forgiveness of our sins, our transgressions, and the iniquities that would give the enemy legal right to our lives.

Cleanse our DNA with your blood and break every curse down our family lines.

Release now unto your children the blessings, favor, and inheritances you have assigned to our hands.

We take authority over every curse of sickness, infirmity, and financial destruction. We bind physical and spiritual destruction, and we release life and that more abundantly.

According to Psalm 102:2, "hide not thy face from us in the day when we are in trouble; incline thine ear unto us: in the day when we call answer us speedily."

Let the root of our lives be purged by the fire of the Holy Spirit and we seal our victory with the blood of Jesus.

In Jesus' name we pray, Amen.

~ Pastor P.M. Finley

GLOBAL PRAYERS

Wisdom to Pray Outside the Box

Proverbs 19:20, Psalm 1:1, Psalm 90:12

Father God, in the name of Jesus, I come before You now God asking You to forgive me for being selfish, for not having the strength and the ability to petition my prayers beyond the four walls of my home and the contents within it. God, I pray for the world and the nation, but the prayers that get my absolute fervor are the ones in the four walls of my box. God, my box has always consisted of my family, immediate needs, children, husband, finances, church, pastor, city, community, emergencies, and You are not pleased. You called us to pray without ceasing, to weep and wale, to petition You fervently, and that our prayers should reach and transform the world. Forgive me for not taking my assignment and running the race that You have set before me.

Lord, thank You for pressing on my heart correction and a desire to change. I pray that You do the same for each individual who reads this prayer. Our eyes are meant to read Your words, our ears are meant to hear the word, and our feet and hands are meant to obey. There is no "wise counsel" apart from You and Your Word. The wise man listens to Your direction, accepts correction and instruction continually.

My prayer today, Father God, is no longer about my four walls, not about my square or its contents. Instead, I seek wise counsel on behalf of our nation and proactively seek out wise counsel on behalf of our government officials. Prick out our hearts to the point where they begin to cry out for what grieves You. Father God, we need You to send Your mercy over the land. Touch the hearts of this nation so that it cries out for all the areas where You are grieved.

Father God, we need You as we've never needed You before! The world has glorified becoming lovers of self, lovers of things, lovers of influence, lovers of material gain, lovers of greed, lovers of sexual immorality, lovers of pride, and thinking of themselves more highly than they aren't. God, I pray that You touch this nation and break the back of every stronghold that hinders people from seeing who You are!

Soften the hardened hearts of the land. Remind them that You are the only true and living God. Remind this nation that it is You who is the wise counsel, that You are the Alpha and the Omega! Remove the scales from the eyes of everyone who does not recognize You for who You are. You are love; You are peace, You are joy, You are righteousness, You are holiness, You are our Redeemer and our Lord! You said in Your word at the name of Jesus, every knee shall bow, and every tongue shall confess. We need You to heal our land! Heal our nation, heal our government and heal Your world! For You reign above all, and I ask this in Jesus's name! Amen.

~Minister A. Lynae Brooks

Heal our Land

Dear God,

We need you! Amid political chaos, social injustice, and a pandemic, we need you. Lord, I come humbly seeking your protection and covering over this land. The United States of America has become divided during crisis and disconnected from you. God, we need your power, your compassion, your love to shower over this country. Open eyes and ears of unbelievers. Prick the hearts of those who say there is no God or whose faith has dissipated. We need you, Lord today more than ever!

Touch the hearts and minds of those who serve in government at all levels who make decisions for our community, our states, and our nation. Guide their thoughts to create policies and procedures that will enhance the lives of all people. Help them to understand the depths of their decisions and to put aside personal feelings, and act in the best interest of all people.

God, please protect our military, public safety and healthcare workers who sacrifice daily so that we can live a better life. Cover them and keep them safe, protected, and healthy as they face each challenge - COVID 19, political unrest in the United States and abroad, protection from foreign enemies and those who threaten harm to our country, state, or community. Provide comfort for their families and return them safely to their loved ones.

In the midst of social injustice and the continual fight for equity and equality, God, help us to be open and willing to accept and celebrate the differences of our sisters and brothers. Illuminate our unconscious biases so that every man, woman, boy and girl can recognize offensive behavior and how others should be treated. The United States is known as a melting pot that welcomes all races, nationalities, creeds, and religions. Replace hate with love and ignorance with understanding and respect. Help us to be a nation that loves God and our brothers and sisters unconditionally. I pray for the day when everyone is treated fairly and equally, not based on how they look or where they come from but because we are all God's children.

COVID 19 has changed and continues to affect life as we know it. We have experienced an enormous loss of life and sickness during the COVID 19 pandemic, but our trust remains in You. As we go through, yes, we will get through, let us lean and depend on you. Let our faith not waiver but grow stronger.

Comfort those who have lost loved ones, strengthen, and heal those who are sick. Times of plague and disease are mentioned in Your Word, Lord, and just like you brought others out, we know you will give us what we need to endure this trying time. We proclaim victory over COVID 19!

Lord God, we need you! We give you praise and thank you for hearing our petitions. We call these things done in Jesus' name. Amen.

~Amanda B. Sumiel

Prayer for those in Authority

Matthew 7:7-8; 2 Timothy 2:1-3; Psalms 24:1; Psalms 5:12

Father God, you said in Your word that if we ask, it will be given to us; if we seek, we will find, and if we knock, the door will be opened. Father, today, I'm seeking, I'm knocking and I thank You in advance that the doors are opened. I come to intercede on behalf of our government. Father, You command us to pray for those in authority over us according to 2 Timothy 2:1-3 that it may be well with us. I lift up the President and Vice President to You. I lift up every elected and appointed official in our land. Father, I thank You that You have rule over each of them. I pray that all those in authority would come to know You. Surround each person in authority with Godly men and women who will give them wise counsel.

Father, I also lift up those in authority in our educational system. I pray that there would be an open heaven over our schools. Father, I pray that discipline and respect be restored in our schools. I pray that our schools would become institutions of transformation where our children would be equipped with knowledge and understanding. Father, send Your Spirit into the hearts and minds of legislators and justices who make laws and rules that directly affect the education system. I pray that our school board members would have wisdom and courage to make decisions that bring order. Father, empower those who write curriculum with truth and give them wisdom to incorporate that wisdom into the material.

Father, I lift up our economic system. The earth is yours and the fullness thereof. I take authority over every demonic spirit, every principality and every spirit of wickedness in our economic system. I command every unclean spirit to lose its hold on the economic system of this world. Father, I declare you are Lord over all these systems. Strategically place Your children in each system to bring change for Your glory. Give them boldness to stand for truth. Let Your favor surround them like a shield. I give you thanks in advance for change to break out throughout the world. In the name of Jesus I pray, amen.

God's Promise for Deliverance

The righteous cry out, and

The Lord hears,

And delivers them out of all their troubles.

Psalms 34:17

Then they cried out to the Lord

in their trouble,

And He delivered them out of their distresses.

Psalms 107:6

~Bridgette L. Threat

Father, Save Our Youth

Lord God, I come to you on behalf of our youth, Lord God. The streets are hemorrhaging from the bloodshed of our young people. Father God, we need you more now than we've ever needed you before.

We need young people to know that their lives matter, God. We need them to understand that there is a future available to them. They just have to want it. In the name of Jesus, I rebuke the spirit of death that is trying to extinguish their light. I rebuke the spirit of hopelessness that a lot of our young people feel. Lord, I pray that You would show them their greatness and allow them to have a glimpse of what their lives could be if they just hold on.

I rebuke the spirit that does not value life. There is a spirit amongst them that doesn't want our young people to grow up into the potential that we know they have. I pray, Heavenly Father, that as the Saints of God, we would set a better example for our young people so that they will

believe that they have something to live for. We must stop judging them by their appearance and actions, and start looking at their hearts, and see them in the light that you see them, Lord. Let us stop asking what's wrong with them and instead try to find out *what happened to them*.

It is my sincere prayer that our babies will put down their guns and pick up the Sword, which is the Word of God. Father, let them seek your face and walk in your wisdom as they settle disputes. Let them stop being so quick to take lives that they aren't the giver, nor the sustainer of. Father, we know that You sent Your Son into this world so that we could have life more abundantly.

You didn't send Jesus here to condemn us, but to Save us, and that is the message that we must get out to our young people. So many of our youth are rejecting you based on the behavior of some of our "Seasoned Saints." Lord, please speak to the hearts and minds of your people so that we can love this generation so relentlessly, that when they experience us, they experience You.

Let us be bold, let us be fearless, and may the words of our mouths and the meditation of our hearts be acceptable to You as we strive to change the hearts and minds of our young people. It is in Jesus' Name that I say, Amen!

~Minister Michelle Lee

Flowers Can't Grow Bigger in Small Pots

We say the prayers, we walk in faith, yet the world is still suffering. Are we so disconnected that we only think about ourselves? Would God be disappointed that our prayers only focus on what we need, what we want. God you word says, *"Call on me, come and pray to me, I will listen"* Jeremiah 29:12

If God answered our prayers for the next seven days, would the world be any different? Lord, help my thoughts to expand beyond my brokenness. Help me to take my focus from just me and mine. Do my prayers match up with my faith? It's much more than a mustard seed now, Lord. You are constantly there, holding me, guiding me, loving me. I thank you so much. Faith and prayer go hand and hand. Hebrews 11:1, *"Faith is confidence in what we hope for and assurance about what we don't see."* Faith is all we have at times—knowing that God has a plan and trying not to get in his way of making it happen.

- **F** - Fantastic
- **A** - Adventures
- **I** - In
- **T** - Trusting
- **H** - Him

Lord, you already know my pain. You already know my challenges, my weaknesses. You know my faults, the areas where I still struggle. Yet you continue to send blessings anyway. Your presence is felt. Your will is being sought after. It may be hard at times, but progress is seen. Now it's time to grow. Time to expand the fence. Time to show you that your babe in Christ has finally grown up. My work with you will no longer be just about the situations right now. My faith knows, you already have that worked out. It's time to serve you, Lord. Help your people more, Lord. Show others the work being done in this broken vessel. The goal is always to honor you, to make you proud, Lord, to show you inside of me. Thank you, Lord. Because of you, this is true; Happiness is on the horizon. Love will come this way again. Emptiness is packing its bags and everlasting joy is signing the papers to live here forever.

From this day forward, the prayers will be bolder, the visions will be expanded. You have done a good work right here; now the favors shall be returned. Thank you for the opportunity. Thank you for creating this warrior and supplying the equipment. Its time. Watch out world. We're coming to take you back!

~Terry Wedlock

Place God Over Greed

1 Timothy 6:10, James 5:1-6, Ecclesiastics 5:10, Mark 8:36

Dear God, we need You to move on behalf of our nation. Our country and this world are in a season where profit and greed take precedence over human lives. The pharmaceutical and health care industries believe they are entitled to put profit before the health or wellbeing of a patient. As a result of their greed and desire for power, their hearts have hardened and ears deafened to those in desperate need. Father God, You hear the cry of every elderly person struggling to decide between paying for medicine or food. I ask You to hear the scream of every person riddled with disease, sickness, infection, and often have to choose between eating, providing for their families, or paying for a prescription. "For what profits a man to gain the world and lose his soul."

Father God, I come right now and in the name of Jesus against the spirit of greed. I pray in the name of Jesus for the nation that You begin to change the minds and hearts of those in leadership. God, allow our government and regulatory officials to look with Your eyes at the immoral actions in the pharmaceutical companies and the healthcare system, and purge them with hyssop! I am pleading on behalf of every person in this world caught in this vicious trap! I'm praying in the name of Jesus for our nation that people would begin to cry out for Your wisdom, and not just any wisdom but Your transformative manifold wisdom. Let it fall upon this nation, upon our government, upon the White House, upon the Food and Drug Administration, and to fall upon the Department of Health and Human Services until they invoke immediate changes!

You said the wealth of the wicked was laid up for the just, but You also said in Your Word that the love of money is the root of all evil. God, I pray right now and in the name of Jesus that You bind up that spirit of lust for money and the spirit of greed. That spirit that it's never enough, that spirit that I would sell my soul for the right price! I decree and declare in the name of Jesus that You flip this over and turn it upside down. Make the wrong right!

Lord, we stamp upon every dollar in God we trust. Some put their trust in men, some in my chariots, but Your people, put our trust in You! God help this nation not just write it on our money but also on our hearts that we trust You. You told us to hide Your word in our hearts that we might not sin against You. The world has sinned against You! We have insulted You, we have turned our backs on You, we have made gods out of money, out of people, out of political parties and political platforms, and out of banks. Jehovah Elohim, the only true and living God!

Teach this nation, have mercy on this world, and pour out Your wisdom over us, pour out Your compassion, forgive us of our greed, forgive us for making any idol a god in our lives. Transform our hearts! Give this nation another chance Lord, to get it right. Jehovah El Shaddai, give this world another opportunity to put You first. We love You, Lord, with all our heart, and we place no one or nothing above You. In Jesus's name, I pray! Amen.

~Minister A. Lynae Brooks

Covering Our Communities

For where two or three gather in my name, there am I with them. Matthew 18:20

Dear Lord,

I come to you on behalf of our community. Father, many of our people are frustrated, sad, afraid, and tired. Our communities are being ravaged by drugs, addictions, violence, and other criminal activity. So many among us are feeling the impact of the pain that is being inflicted within our communities.

God, we need you to intervene on our behalf. You told us that if we who are called by your name would humble ourselves and pray and seek your face, that you would hear from heaven. Our land is sick and needs the type of cleansing and healing that can only come from you. This is not a task for any earthly mortal. This is a job for your God. Therefore, we ask you to come through for us, Jesus! We cannot make it through without you.

We pray against every demonic attack that has risen against our communities and neighborhoods. We plead the blood of Jesus over addiction, bad habits, alcoholism, sex trafficking, molestation, domestic violence, and vandalism. We also come against violence, murder, and destructive behaviors. We pray for those who have lost hope and faith in you.

Some among us have lost faith in community. We lift those who feel as though no one loves them. We ask you to restore broken relationships, Lord. We ask you to show us to resolve conflicts amicably and without malice. We pray that you send someone who will show the love of your Son Jesus Christ so that they feel your love and commit their lives to you.

We pray for those who have lost faith in you. Draw your people closer to you, Lord. We ask you to send revival into our communities. Anoint your mouthpieces to preach your word so that healing and deliverance come. Let the fire of the Holy Ghost fall upon us so that we can move forward cleansed and with a new vitality and abundant life.

We pray for those who have the task to protect and serve the members of our communities. May they embody the spirit of servanthood and not entitlement. We ask you to bless them as they serve your people and make them a blessing.

We cover our communities in the blood of Jesus. We ask you, Lord to help us so we don't have to live in fear. We pray for every person who is afraid to leave their home. We also lift those who are afraid while inside theirs. We reassure them through Isaiah 54:17, no weapon that is formed against them will succeed. May they find peace in this promise.

God, we thank you in advance for sending help to our communities. We bless you for healing. We give you glory for setting people free from bondage. We praise you in advance for victory in our communities, in Jesus' name. Amen!

~Evangelist Teraleen R. Campbell

A Prayer for the Church

Dear Heavenly Father,

Thank you for your love, your understanding, and your long-suffering towards us. Thank you for your only begotten son, Jesus Christ, my Lord and my savior. Thank you for the gift of salvation. Thank you for your mercy on our souls, Father. Father, you are all-powerful, completely amazing, and totally in control, and I am grateful to have the privilege to speak to you, that you would incline your ear to hear from me and that I would have the petition that I ask of you. Thank you for being concerned about the things that concern me and knowing what I have need of even before I ask. Thank you for providing for me all things that pertain to life and godliness. Thank you for the way that you care for me, being meticulous and detailed in every way, giving me good gifts always. Father, I thank you that I can cast my worries on you because you provide for me.

So, Father, because of who you are, how awesome you are, how much you love us, I ask Lord that the desires of your heart be fulfilled. Knowing that your desire is not that any man should perish, but that all would come to repentance, and knowing that the harvest is plentiful, yet the laborers are few. Father, I pray right now, in the name of Jesus that you would send forth the laborers.

Teach us how to work in your vineyard, O' Lord. Provide us with your wisdom for winning souls for your kingdom. You've told us that he who wins souls is wise, and any man that asks for wisdom, you would give it liberally. So, Father, I pray, in the name of Jesus, that you would freely give wisdom to your children to win souls for you. Stir in each and every one of your children a desire in our hearts to be about our Father's business, no longer caring for the things of this world, but with our hearts and minds set on things above. Teach us your ways that we may grow and mature in the way and are prepared and available for your use.

Teach us how to disciple the babes in Christ that they may grow and mature, and the growth of the body of Christ is continual from generation to generation. Let there be families of people that know you and do exploits for generations to come, should the Lord tarry.

I pray for your church to look like what you desire it to look like, filled with love and compassion, walking in peace and speaking the truth, and encouraging one another in your word. I pray for the body of Christ to be whole, without spot, wrinkle, blemish or any such thing, each child completely free, standing on your word, immovable, filled with faith and obedient in every way. Help us to be transformed to a people that examine themselves and are quick to repent, humbling ourselves under your mighty hand, fully submitted, patient and steadfast. Thank you, Lord, for the transformation that is coming. In Jesus name, I pray. Amen.

~Mya Jackson Brown

Healing for the World

Lord, I come to you today, crying out for our world. Lord, this world needs you like never before. Every inch of land and sea, from the skyline to the grass line, everything you have placed on this earth, we need a healing. Our land is running rampant with disease, drugs, mental, physical, and spiritual illnesses. God, we need your healing hands to graze across this globe we call Earth. God, touch the minds of everyone that dwells in your land. Free us from the noise that drowns out your voice. Help us to tune our ears in to what you are saying to us. Touch our hearts God. Make it clean and renew within us the right spirit; a spirit of love and kindness, forgiveness and humility.

God wipe this earth from the north, south, east, and west of all the drugs that pollute not only the adults but our children. Help us to learn to come together as people to help one another and keep our communities clean. As a people, we shouldn't be creating things that keep us down but to create things to keep each other lifted up. Your word says there is life and death in the tongue, so help us to speak life into others instead of spewing words or negativity. Words that cut deep to a person's soul, words that may make or break an individual.

God rid us of cancer, diabetes, strokes, sickle cell, Down syndrome, COVID, and any other disease that seeks to destroy people and families. God, destroy every scientific lab created to brew up disease for population control. Put a stop to the purchase of guns and gun violence. God, I ask that you stop wars against nations and wars in our very own communities. Dispel the power of gangs and cultic activity and anything else that thinks it has the power to take over someone's mind and body.

Break chains for us today, God. Break strongholds in our land. Bring us to leave God so that we can carry out the work you have called each of us to do. God, I come up against the enemy, the prince of the airways and the tactics put in place to brainwash our children with the music that is being created to control their minds. Music all over the world is being strategically made to make sure perversion and violence are the things guiding our children and others to keep them from knowing You and getting closer to You, to have that intimate relationship with you, God. God, fill the people of your land with a burning desire to want to seek your face and turn from their wicked ways. Help us to get on one accord as a people. Help the intercessors all over this world to rise up and take heed to the assignment given to us. God help us to be everything you have called us to be. God, you are awesome, and I thank you in advance for the turn around that is to come for Your land. In Jesus name, Amen!

~Minister Angelique M. Bullock

PETITION PRAYERS

CONVERSATIONS WITH GOD: WAITING

But those who hope in the Lord will renew their strength. They will soar on wings like eagles; they will run and not grow weary, they will walk and not faint. Isaiah 40:31

Lord, please help me to learn to wait on you, especially in my times of frustration, when I grow weary because I don't see the light at the end of the tunnel. You are truly the Author and Finisher of my Faith, and I know that you can do all things except fail. Your timing is perfect, and what you have for me is for me. Help me to wait on you in the times that I want to give up because I wonder if my efforts are futile. Lord, I know that when a seed is planted, it has to be cultivated; it has to be in fertile ground, it has to be watered, and it has to have time to grow. I may not know what is happening underground, but I believe that something is happening, and in time there will be a crop.

Just like the runner in a race, I pray that you would give me endurance to run on and see what the end will bring. Father, I realize that I won't always be the first one to cross the finish line, but I can still finish the race strong if I keep my mind stayed on you. Lord, I realize that in life, slow and steady still finishes well. Let me be ever mindful of that so that when things don't happen in the timing that I think they should, I will still trust in you and your timing. I trust in you because I know that you do all things well. Lord, please forgive me for the times that I seem to forget that. Lord, I love you, and I place nothing and no one above you. Thank you for keeping me moving forward when I want to give up. Thank you, Lord, for pushing me when I want to give in to my weariness. Help me to soar high above my problems like an Eagle, and to remember that if you bring me to any situation, you will help me through the situation. Amen.

~Minister Michelle Lee

Prayer to Be Released from the Stronghold of a Toxic Relationship

Father God; in the name of your precious son Jesus,

I come to you Lord right now, thanking you for another day to see your glory. Thank you for every blessing, no matter how big or small

Thank you, Father God, for your grace which sustains me day to day.

Father, I come to you humbly, Lord, asking you to release me from this marriage.

Lord, you know my husband's addiction better than me, and Lord, I cannot say no to him in my own strength.

Release me, oh Lord.

Father, you are Almighty and through your strength, Lord, I give this marriage back to you. I give this stronghold of addiction back to you

I give this Godly man who knows your way Lord, back to you. Cover him, Father God.

Heal him, Lord.

Father, remind him of who YOU are, God, and through you, Lord, all things are possible through your son Christ who strengthens us, Lord.

And Father, when the victory report comes out that he is delivered from addiction, Lord, let us give you the victory in this matter.

Let him go back into the streets with a clean heart and renewed mind with a testimony to deliver souls to you, Lord.

Finally, Lord, work on me, Lord. Show me your will for my life in this season

Father. Strengthen me to be the best mother to these children.

Let them see you when they see me.

Lord, for the time I have lost tarrying within this addicted relationship, restore everything that I lost in my finances, my faith and my strength. Thank you in advance for your strength and your power, in the name of your son Jesus and his awesome sacrifice I pray, Amen.

~Cassandra Epps

For the Single Woman

Lord,

I come to you as humbly as I know, asking you to carry me, support me, and undergird me when I feel weak. During the times that I feel alone, please remind me that You will never leave me nor forsake me. When I wonder what lies ahead, reassure me that You are the author and finisher of my faith. When I'm feeling lost, send those sweet reminders that You order my steps and even count the precious hairs on my head. As I navigate this world alone, let me never feel lonely but find my confidence and trust in You. Send laborers across my path to minister to me on the rough days and cheer me on during the good days. Let none of my efforts be for naught as I follow Your lead. Guide my steps, bridle my lips and lead the way, so I can remain safe and sound in you.

Surround me with the right people at the right time who will love me, support me, and encourage me. Give me the right words to say as I minister to others….may they not see me, but You on the inside of me. Grant me peace that passes all understanding that can only be found in You. Remind me daily that You know my end from my beginning and that all things work together for the good of those who love You and are called according to Your purpose. May your light shine brightly to all those around me and may my life serve as a testimony of your faithfulness and the fulfillment of Your promises. In Jesus name, I pray.

~Dr. Toyia K. Younger

Prophetic Ignition

Father God, in the name of Jesus, thank you for allowing us to have access to your presence. To be able to access the heavenly realm freely. Being created to worship you, God in spirit and in truth, is a blessing. Our desire is to hear clearly what your spirit is saying. Deafen our ears to the noise and voices that contradict your word. Open our prophetic ear gates so that your supernatural realm download may begin. As we receive instructions, and heavens, eventual plans and purposes invade earth, align us in thought and deed to your divine precepts. Let us proclaim what your spirit is saying throughout the Earth. Father, deploy your prophets to accelerate in your prophetic frequency. To decree and declare and dissolve doubt with heavenly accuracy. Lord, strip every spirit of fear that is being used by the enemy to cause prophetic paralysis among your chosen vessels. Father, as we begin to take territory in the regions in which you have assigned, God, we release the breaker anointing to go before us and forcefully shatter the stony ground in the land and hardened hearts of the people. Ignite a fire throughout the earth to provoke man to live holy once again. I decree and declare the fresh wind of the Lord Jesus Christ will dismantle every demonic snare, hindrance, bondage and delay the enemy initiated. As we pursue this next dimension of prophetic charge, we invite the Holy Spirit to release unto us a greater anointing to further the Kingdom agenda. In the Mighty Name of Jesus, Amen.

~Nicki Nichols

A Praying Man's Covering

Father in the name of Jesus. I come to you humble, thankful, grateful and with no pride in my heart. Heavenly Father, I thank you for this time and this moment with You. Lord, I ask you to look down from your throne in the heavens. To look through the stars and the moon to see us here on earth. I ask you, Lord, that you touch, bless, anoint, and appoint each man on this earth to be God serving men. Lord touch, mold, and shape his heart, his mind and his spirit so that he does not conform to the pattern of this world, but be transformed by the renewing of their mind. Then you will be able to test and approve what God's will is-his good, pleasing and perfect will. Show and reveal to him that he's not only a father, but he's also a spiritual teacher and leader in his household, a mentor to his children and other children, to some he will be the one that others will want to be like and people they select in their lives, a provider and much more to his spouse, children, and family. Lord, keep him strong in his faith, honest, a person of the highest integrity, a person of patience, and of endurance; Lord, continue to have him be a prayerful man who covers his family while in their presence and beyond the sights and sounds of his eyes. God show and reveal to him the difference between a God-serving man, a serving-man, a man, and a boy. That he will be the protector and provide the protection and coverage that is needed for a strong and covered household. God, may he always praise you, honor you, adore you, in times of great strength and even in his times of weakness. May he trust you and have faith in you in his time of seeking your guidance in his life and decisions. It is in Jesus' name that I ask of these prayers, for you are a loving and faithful God all the days of my life. In Jesus' name Amen.

~Brian Pinson

Time for Financial Breakthrough

"Beloved, I wish above all things that thou mayest prosper and be in health, even as thy soul prospereth." 3 John 1:2

Thank you, oh God, for your listening ear and for access to your throne. God, I bless you, for what is man that you are mindful of us? God, I thank you that I belong to Christ and am, therefore, the seed of Abraham. In accordance with Gal. 3:29, the blessings of Abraham and his promised covenant are upon me. Your steadfast love and covenant are with me because I love and obey you, and I am blessed even to a thousand generations, according to Deut. 7:9.

Lord, because it is You that gives me the power to get wealth, according to Duet. 8:18, I pray that you would give me million-dollar money-making ideas, witty and innovative inventions, cutting edge and generational wealth-producing strategies. Lord, even as I sleep, give me downloads of business plans, blueprints, and strategies. Let wealth and riches be drawn to my hands and everything that I touch prosper in the name of Jesus.

I know, Lord, that you desire for me to prosper from the inside out according to 3 John 1:2. Lord, fix me on the inside. Let me possess inner health, wholeness, and wealth so that prosperity in the material realm will also be my portion.

I renounce, come out of agreement with and release myself from word curses that I have spoken, such as, "I'm broke, I don't have any money, and I'm poor. I call for a crop failure of these words now, in the name of Jesus.

I plead the blood of Jesus over my mind. I arrest, cause to cease and desist and dispel all thoughts of mediocrity, impoverishment and lack. For I seek You Lord and therefore I will not lack any good thing, according to Ps. 34:10.

You have protected me in Goshen even as you did with the children of Israel and given me a land of milk and honey. Because I am your servant, You take pleasure in my prosperity, according to Ps. 35:27. All of my needs are met, and I am blessed so that I can bless others. Give me wisdom, Lord, so that the seed you give me is sown only in fertile ground, for You have given me the seed to sow. According to 2 Cor 9:10.

I seal this prayer with the Word of God, which shall never return void, but do exactly what it is sent out to do. I seal this prayer with the Blood of Jesus, which covers me and gives me a direct hotline to heaven, the angels, and my heavenly Father. And I seal this prayer with the Name of Jesus because whatever I ask for in Jesus' name, believing, I shall have it. I also dispatch warrior angels into the heavenly realm to battle against any demonic force that would try to hold up, hinder, delay or obstruct the manifestation of this prayer from speedily coming forth, in Jesus' name. Amen!!

~Elder Elect Sonja Owens

Prayer to Increase My Discernment

Father God, the author, and finisher of my faith.

Lord, I come to you in the name of your son Jesus to first thank you for another day of life. Thank you, father, for another opportunity to call on your name.

Lord, you said in your word that you would never leave us or forsake us. I need you right now.

Lord, I come asking you to show me what your will is for me.

Let not my spirit of discernment be tainted by the ways of this world. Reveal to me what you have for me.

Give me the power to separate what is meant for good from what the enemy would have as a snare for me.

Cover me in the blood of Jesus, as I move through this life. Increase my faith, Lord.

Remove any anxiety in my spirit.

Cover me with your grace and when I fail you will cover me with your mercy—thanking you in advance, Lord.

Amen.

~Cassandra Epps

THE TABERNACLE PRAYER

THE BRAZEN ALTAR- The place of sacrifice

Through your sacrifice, dear Jesus, I am declared righteous. Through your blood, my sins are forgiven.

Dear Jesus, you took away my infirmities and carried away all my weakness. Therefore, sickness is illegal in my body.

According to Galatians 3:13, Christ hath redeemed me from the curse of the law, and through your blood, I have been redeemed from death, hell and the grave.

THE LAVER- The place of washing

We see our lives in the reflection of the Word of God. And as we look at the ten commandments, if we have violated your laws and sinned against you in any area, we repent and receive the refreshing and cleansing power of your word.

THE CANDLESTICK

As I walk into the Holy Place, the place of wisdom and understanding, I ask you, Holy Spirit, to give me wisdom and help me to solve all my problems. Give me your tremendous might so that I may heal the sick and cast out devils.

THE TABLE OF SHOWBREAD

I thank you for the word of God. from Genesis to Revelation.
I thank you for the logos- the written word of God
I thank you for the rhema- the inspired word of God
Holy Spirit, I ask that you to turn the logos into rhema that I may manifest in the earth.

THE ALTAR OF INCENSE- The praise of the saints.

Most holy father, we praise you and glorify your name because you are:

- **Omnipotent**- You are all-powerful
- **Omnipresent**- You are present everywhere
- **Omniscient**- You are all-knowing

I will not worry or become afraid, but I will cast my cares upon you according to yourword.

THE ARK OF THE COVENANT

Through the blood of Jesus, the sins of the world have been redeemed and paid off.

The blood of Jesus on the mercy seat- disarms sickness, disarms disease, disarms fear of failure, and disarms the fear of running out.

According to Mark 11:24, the things that we have desired we believe that we receive, and we have them now in Jesus name, Amen.

~Rev. P.M. Finley

You Were Always There

Lord, we come to you in need of prayer. Few words have been spoken. All thoughts and feelings were brought only to you. No one else could help but you. The pain was so raw no one could handle it but you. God, only someone as merciful as you could move her pass the thoughts of ending her pain, taking her life, making everything go away. You stepped in when she needed it the most. Thank you for allowing her to see that her time here is not coming to an end but instead a new beginning. The temporary heartache will never outweigh a mother's love. You kept telling her that she was loved even when she could not see it nor feel it. You kept showing her how to walk with you step by step. How to trust in you day by day. How to pray to you night after night, never leaving her alone. Her wounds are still deep, painful to move forward, but she is ready. She is ready to do the work you require. Actively and openly pursuing you, Lord. Lord, she is ready to step back into her community, where she can grow surrounded by your angels placed around her. Transparency is a blessing. Being open and honest with herself is necessary in order to begin to heal. The journey may not be easy, but she will never feel alone again.

You were always there. Twenty-six years ago, your presence was felt when her oldest child was young. You stepped in and saved them. Whispering to her, "I have a purpose for you." On a snowy day, the car spun out of control. You safely placed the car in the grass. She was amazed how no other cars crashed into them. That was you, God, and she knew it. Lord, you put something inside of her that day. Yet, she did not know what to do with it, but the candle had been lit. God, please forgive her. She never knew how to balance everything and still made time for you. She kept getting in your way. She tried to be everything for everyone. Wearing a mask of strength to hide her fear and unwillingness to surrender. She was about to be in the biggest fight for her life! God, thank you. You moved everything she held close to her heart out of view. You needed her to see and focus on only you. You were her father, you were her strength, you were her provider.

You were always there. She wanted her pride to be enough, her independence to be enough, her anger to be enough. But it was not. Lord, you watched as she fought you to hold on to what she had, but you kept shaking things up by working in her. She tried to fix things as she always did, yet things got worse. That was you again, working in her. She had to let go, to trust your process in order to save herself, to love herself. God, you finally had her all to yourself. Showing her how to lean on you. How to put your will in front of her own. Trusting you, not on what she felt or thought. Not allowing Satan to control her eyes, her mind, her reactions to life. She learned how to be silent, how to wait for direction, how to listen and take correction from you, Lord. How to be grateful, content and satisfied. You allowed her to revise her surroundings to match her new focus. Rooms of anger became rooms of progress. Rooms of sadness became new visions of hope. Lord, while you were transforming her from the inside, you were blessing her to transform her surroundings as well. Changes were needed so a peaceful healing could begin. Her past molded her, but you were reshaping her, renewing her. Allowing her to see herself through your eyes. You were not in the background of her life anymore; you were now right in front.

You were always there even when she did not know she needed you. Properly moving through life with a family, she did not know how to manage gracefully, she did not know how to manage finances responsibly, and feeling she did not know how to express painlessly, everything always felt so hard. There was always so much that needed to be done. She often felt alone, unloved and unappreciated. She wanted to be everything to everyone, often dropping the ball or moving based on obligation instead of love. Lord, your guidance was absent from her life. Now your presence shows her how to be humble, how to listen more and speak less. How to parent with a forgiving heart, using her words to uplift instead of tearing down. God, you showed her how to be softer, how to let the walls of fear, anger, stubbornness, bitterness, selfishness, and pride down. You gave her the promise of your protection. She was always searching for something, trying to fill it with stuff, nothing tangible. Now she is searching for you. How to make you proud, how to learn more about you, how to follow your words. Thank you for the relocation, seeing where change needs to occur. Let the pruning continue. Thank you.

~Terry Wedlock

Prayer for Single Parents

Heavenly Father, I come to you as humbly as I know how to thank you for everything that you have done. God, I thank you for the gift of children and the gift of being a parent. God, I come specifically for those who are carrying the weight of the parenting responsibility alone. God, I ask that you comfort them like only you can. God, your Word says that the step of those who are righteous are ordered by you. So, God, I come right now to ask that you order their steps. God, I ask that you make any crooked paths straight. God, I ask that you comfort them when they cry out in the midnight hours. God, I ask that you uphold them with your right hand. Yes, God, your right hand of power and authority. God, I ask that you give your manifested favor in their lives. God, I declare a financial breakthrough over their homes. I decree that you would hold no good thing from them. God, I declare that your will for their lives would be crystal clear to them as they make decisions for their families. God, I speak to their loneliness and disappointments. God, I ask that you breathe over their lives. Breathe just like you did in the valley of dry bones. God, breathe over their neglected dream. Breathe over their aspirations. God, breathe into their careers and businesses. God minister to the inner darkness that is hidden. God walk with them, talk with them, incline your ears to them and their ears to you. Allow them to have an encounter with you like never before. Allow them to see you with new eyes and to hear you with new ears. God let the words of their mouths and the meditation of their hearts be acceptable in your sight. God, we ask all these things in Jesus' name, Amen.

~Minister Dunia Kambon-Thornton

YOU WATCHED US

We met and fell in love, you watched us. We played house and made a family, you watched us. The dress was bought, the tux was rented, we thought we saw you there. You kept calling our names, we were not listening. You kept knocking on the door for us to let you in, we ignored you. Not sure if you kept talking to him as you were to me, but little changed. Even when we did not do our part, you still did yours. You protected the family, you kept everyone safe, yet we still made you sit and wait some more. We would come to you only to walk away again and again. You still loved us. You surrounded us with family and friends that knew your word, we saw them. You took us to places where your word was spoken, we listened and still walked away. Lord, you watched us struggle with our words to one another, the attention we did not show, the love we did not know how to express and the hurt feeling we did not know how to deal with. We looked good from the outside, but you -knew the truth. Lord, we never let you in to take the lead, to stand in front of us and take the lead. We constantly played tug of war with words, power and pain. You allowed us to make mistakes, always right there to help, yet we seldom asked. You helped us through health scares, family illnesses and unforeseen deaths. We still thought we would be alright with you in the background. You allowed us to take the lead as the parents of the home. You watched us mistakenly focus more on discipline than showing love. You watched us treat each other based on how we felt instead of friends. You saw me walk toward you many times, only to retreat when times got hard. Following you always seemed to hurt. Looking at yourself, seeing your flaws, denying yourself. It was too hard, Lord. Watching my tongue, being fast to listen and slow to respond. Being a good helpmate and partner. Not wanting to be in control. Not falsely thinking of ways to fix everyone's problems. That was a parent's job, right? Now 20 years later, it's all gone. No marriage, no family under one roof, no healthy communication between anyone. Why didn't we let you show us? Show us how to come to you in prayer for direction. Show us how to love each other as you love us. Father, forgive us for thinking we knew what was best. We were wrong. We built our lives around worldly beliefs when you were all we ever needed.

~Terry Wedlock

Covering Those Who Care - Prayer for Caregivers

> *Don't worry about anything; instead, pray about everything. Tell God what you need and thank him for all he has done. Then you will experience God's peace, which exceeds anything we can understand. His peace will guard your hearts and minds as you live in Christ Jesus.*
> *Philippians 4:6-7 NLT*

Dear God, I come to you on behalf of those who serve in the role of caregiver. Lord, you know the responsibility that has been placed in their hands. You know the weight of their current assignment.

It is with this in mind that I intercede on their behalf. God, you see the sleepless nights, the loneliness, the anxiety, the depression, and other rollercoaster of emotions that they feel. Understanding that you are the omniscient God, I ask that you allow them to feel your presence. During their lonely moments, please remind them that they are never alone.

I cover them as they make decisions that will impact both them and the person for whom they are caring. May they always seek you first. I ask you to give them a greater level of wisdom for this assignment. I come against guilt as a result of their decisions.

I pray for their families. I come against any resentment that some may feel. Please don't allow that to turn into bitterness. I pray against family turmoil and conflicts that seem irreconcilable. Help them to resolve conflicts, Lord. Release a spirit of understanding and healthy communication. I bind the hand of the devil that seeks to infiltrate families and turn husbands, wives, and siblings against each other.

Father, let love abide and let homes be sanctuaries of your peace.

God, I pray for the moments of weariness. Please sustain them during these times. May their due season come and be more than they imagined. Until that time, God, I ask you to encourage their hearts, especially on days when their loved one is combative, uncooperative or does not recognize them.

Lord, I pray that you give them strength during their weakest moments.

Help them to go on even when they want to give up. Send help, even if it comes from the most unlikely source. Please release resources that will help support and sustain those who have committed to providing care.

Bless them financially, Father. I ask that you do not allow them to go lacking for any good and necessary thing. I decree and declare that caregivers will lack nothing- health-wise, financially, or mentally.

Lord, I pray that you allow them to remain true to you and to themselves. Grant precious time to steal away for times of self-care and renewal. Give them extended moments with you. Speak to them and refresh their souls. Remind them that they are more than conquerors and that you do love them.

I ask kind Father that you help every caregiver to manage their emotions, especially when receiving adverse doctor's reports and diagnoses. I pray that you give them patience when dealing with healthcare professionals and facility staff. Perfect their communication skills so they can convey concerns and ask questions to get answers as they provide care, Lord.

Finally, Lord, I ask that you stabilize my caregiving brothers and sisters. On days when anxiety, fear and depression attack them, and it feels as though the ground is sinking from under them, I pray that you enable them to feel the stability of your love. Most of all, remind them that you care for them. This is my prayer in Jesus' name, Amen.

~Evangelist Teraleen R. Campbell

Blessing and Favor

Eternal and wise God, we come to you today just to say thank you. We thank you for being a good Father. We call you Abba. We are your children and your heir. All is yours, and you are a Father that gives good gifts to your children. We thank you for life, health, and strength. We thank you for the use of our limbs, our parts, and members. We thank you for all you do in the lives of your people. We thank you for being the King of kings and Lord of lords. We thank you for being a God of wonders. We thank you for being Lord. You are the great "I AM." There is no one besides You. You are powerful and full of majesty. We marvel at all your creation. You are the God of Israel, and we give you praise. God, we confess our sins and ask that you wash us with the blood of Christ. We ask that you wash us from all unrighteousness, anything in us that is not like you. We ask that you wash us until we are clean and make us holy in thy sight. We thank you for your grace and your mercy. We thank you for keeping and guiding us. We thank you for your provision and protection. We thank you for your peace which passes all understanding. We thank you for your word, which we have hid in our hearts that we may not sin against you.

Jehovah Jireh, you provide for the needs of your people. As You provided for Abraham and Isaac, You have provided for me and my family! Thank you for the blessings of Your provisions. You will provide for all our needs for always. Thank You for Your work on the cross that gives me Eternal Life! We ask for your blessings over our home, our families, and children. We ask for you to bless our finances, that we have more than enough. We ask that you give us access to every blocked blessing and every closed door. We want to increase and release from debt. Your word says to owe no man nothing but love. We pray for your favor to follow us and to be a shield to us.

God, we ask that you cover us with your favor, surround us with your favor. Favor to my left, favor to my right, favor in front and favor in back. I wear a coat of favor. We ask for blessing over each and everything that we are attached to God, circumcise our hearts and the hearts of our descendants so that we may love you with all your heart, and with all your soul and live as declared in your word. Give us long life and prosperity in the land as you promised in your word. Go before me and clear the path. You are the Alpha and the Omega, the First and the Last, the Beginning and the End. In you, we have our being. In Jesus name, Amen.

~Minister Melissa Powell-Harrell

Closing Reflection and Prayer

God, every good and perfect gift comes from You, and we can't even fathom what You have in store for us in the future... but we do know that You have already secured it, already paid for it, already laid out a path for us to get it.

God, we want to be where You are. We want to see Your face, to hear Your voice, to be in the very presence of perfect Love. Love undefiled. Love as pure as the cry of a newly born babe.

Come meet the person reading this right where they are at this moment, for You know them completely. You know the struggles, the battles, the failures, and the mountains they are fighting against. You know what is needed to win, and You already have it secured. More than the good gifts You bring to us all, bring Your presence to them right now.

In the tension, in the darkness, in the battle, in the wilderness, we will not stop praising You, worshipping You, crying out for You, trusting You, humbling ourselves to You, and remembering how You have faithfully brought us here.

We wait expectantly for You, O Lord. You are our perfect portion. You are everything we need.

~Holly Magnuson

Reprinted with permission from *Everything I Need,* Bible App Plan

CONTRIBUTING AUTHORS

(in alphabetical order)

Reverend Darryl D. Brookins

Reverend Darryl D. Brookins is a Baltimore native. He is a product of the Baltimore public school system. He holds an undergraduate degree in Chemical Engineering from the University of Delaware, a certificate of Business from the Johns Hopkins University and an M.B.A. in Technology Management from the University of Phoenix.

He is the middle child of three siblings and loves family. Darryl is also an ordained elder in the Church of God in Christ and has been blessed to serve in ministry for 31 years. He comes from a long line of pastors, missionaries, and evangelists. Prayer is a major part of his life. And he enjoys the relationship he has with God.

He has experienced God's miraculous power to heal from congestive heart failure and trusts God's word for his very life. He firmly believes that God's word will perform its intended purpose before it can return to Him (Isaiah 55:11) and that God watches over every word to ensure it does so (Jeremiah 1:12).

Contact: Twitter @dbrookings06

Minister A. Lynae Brooks

Minister A. Lynae Brooks is a woman called by God and is highly passionate about her life's prophetic and intercessory mantles. At the core of A Lynae's heart is the vital need to communicate with God in prayer. She witnessed early as a child, the miracles and deliverance power found in prayer.

Minister Brooks has served alongside her husband, William "Bill" Brooks III, as Ministry Leads for WBF Prison Ministry; collectively, they have ministered to multiple correctional facilities for 25 years and counting. If asked, Prison ministry would be one of her most essential purposes in life. She knows firsthand the transformational impact that prison ministry has on the lives of individuals and families incarcerated.

A native of Baltimore County, Maryland, Minister Brooks is an effervescent woman with a heart for public service. As a Higher Education Technology professional and small business owner, Minister Brooks excels in her career spanning over 19 years.

Accepting the call to Ministry in 2014, Ministry Brooks has served in numerous capacities; from Sunday School Secretary, Dance Ministry Member and Teacher, Intercessory Prayer, Pastor's Aid, Bishop's Executive Administrator, Usher Board, Youth Departments Leader, Media Team, Women of Purpose, Prison Ministry and Missionary In-Training. She is an active member of Walk by Faith Ministries in Baltimore, Maryland, and continues to strive after God's heart.

She is the proud wife and the mother of four fantastic adult children and a grandson. In her leisure time, she enjoys quality time with her family, reading, cooking, listening to music, and above all, fulfilling the will of God is her primary purpose.

Follow Minister A Lynae Brooks:
www.alynaebrooks.com
contact@alynaebrooks.com
{443} 252-3383
IG: a_lynaebrooks

Mya Jackson Brown

Mya Jackson Brown is simply "a woman that is just trying to get things right with God," a wife, mother of three, dog owner, a nurse and small business owner that is an active member in her local congregation. Her relationship with God is her main priority because she knows without it, there is nothing. She loves prayer because it is where she can come into His presence and have a dialogue with Him. In her prayer time, she receives guidance, encouragement, correction, understanding, strength, healing, and all that she needs to continue the journey through life.

Contact: You can connect with Mya on Facebook at facebook.com/myajb

Minister Angelique M. Bullock

Minister Angelique M. Bullock is a teacher of the Baltimore City Public School System. She has a Bachelor's Degree in Hospitality Management from Johnson and Wales University and a Master's of Education Degree in School Improvement Leadership with Administration Certification from Goucher College. Min. Angelique accepted her call to preach in April 2018. Since then, she has been under the leadership of Pastor Damon Dorsey, Walk By Faith Ministries, where she serves as an Associate Minister, teaches Bible Study and serves on the Intercessory Prayer Ministry.

Angelique preached her initial sermon on March 6, 2019. Previous to Walk By Faith Ministries, she served on the Praise Team, Choir, Dance Ministry, Youth and Young Adult Ministry and was the leader of the Step Team at New Antioch Church. Angelique has the support of her loving daughter, Angela Bullock and many other family and friends.

Contact: Facebook @AngeliqueBullock

Lashaviar S. Burns

LaShaviar Burns, a high school Mathematics teacher, who teaches from Algebra 1 to Probability and Statistics with Baltimore City Public Schools. LaShaviar believes that calculations and problem-solving skills are not only a fundamental part of academic excellence but are also the stepping stones of critical thinking in high school and beyond. LaShaviar holds a BS degree in Mathematics and a master's degree in Adult and Continuing Education from Coppin State University. LaShaviar was born, raised, and still resides in Baltimore, MD. She is a member of Walk by Faith Ministries and serves as the leader of the church's outreach ministry (Helping Mankind Ministry). LaShaviar is also a proud member of Delta Psi Epsilon Christian Sorority, Inc. She can be found on Facebook and Instagram as LaShaviar Bums. Finally, prayer is vital because it changes things, and it helps build a relationship with God through verbal and nonverbal communication.

Contact: lashaviar999@yahoo.com

Evangelist Teraleen R. Campbell

An award-winning author, speaker and certified coach, Evangelist Teraleen R. Campbell serves several organizations within her community in the Washington, DC, suburban area. One who knows the worth of prayer, she loves to intercede on behalf of the needs of God's people and serves as lead intercessor each month for a local non-profit organization.

A survivor of childhood domestic abuse, at the hands of her stepfather, Teraleen is a tireless advocate against domestic violence. She participates in events that address this issue. Her community involvement has garnered recognition from professional, faith-based, and non-profit organizations such as the March of Dimes, Be the Match, and Taylor Thomas of WHUR Radio.

Her ministry extends to Zeta Phi Beta Sorority, Inc. She authored the sorority's Centennial Prayer and facilitated the Global Day of Prayer for several years. She also was a co-author for *Faith of Our Founders*, which is the sorority's devotional book.

No stranger to providing encouragement through the written word, Teraleen has co-authored five books. Additionally, she released the award-winning *From Carefree to Caregiver* in 2018. She created Caregivers Connect online support group and has become known as the Caregiver to caregivers. Through this online community, she provides caregivers with resources, support, and valuable information. Her newest release *Embracing Your New Normal Devotional*, provides support after the loss of a loved one.

> Website - Teraleencampbell.com
> Facebook, Twitter & Instagram - Teraleen Campbell

Cassandra Epps

Since relocating to Charlotte, NC in 2007 from Baltimore, MD, Ms. Epps has worked as a Senior Consultant for various companies. She also served as adjunct faculty at the undergraduate and graduate school levels.

She is an active member of Delta Sigma Theta, Inc., where she mentors young ladies. She made a natural transition from the Human Resources profession to an IT Professional, by developing and maintaining databases for HR data. That transition has launched her career into the Information Technology space, where she works as a Program Manager.

Ms. Epps makes herself available voluntarily to assist many non-profit organizations. She loves her church which is the platform where she launched her skills as a prayer intercessor. Her spirit of discernment guides her daily life.

Ms. Epps has a Master of Science in Human Resources Management and Organizational Development from the Johns Hopkins University and a Bachelor of Science degree in Finance from the Towson University. She currently attends Emory University School of Law to attain a Juris Master's degree, spring 2022.

In her spare time, she enjoys spending time with her two beautiful daughters Kayla and Kaylin. She loves to travel, sing, play tennis and read when time permits. Her happy place is anywhere near the water.

Contact: Facebook : Cassandra Epps Kincaid
IG: Cassandra Epps Kincaid

Pastor P.M. Finley

Paul M. Finley is the Founder and Pastor of the Lion of Judah Worship Center Church of God in Christ, where his mission is to "take the name of Jesus Christ to the nations, through the power of the Holy Ghost."

Pastor Finley currently functions as the Episcopal Adjutant to the Bishop Joel H. Lyles, General Secretary of the Church of God in Christ and was named the Chairman of AIM for Greater Maryland First Jurisdiction. Previously, he served as the President for the Department of Evangelism and Vice President of the Sunday School Department.

Pastor Finley's focus for ministry is to see souls saved, bodies healed, and souls delivered from the enemy's oppression. He is heeding God's call to have a local, national, and international ministry with the establishment of P. M. Finley Ministries, a non-profit ministry focused on spreading the unconditional love and healing power of Jesus Christ to our hurting nation and world.

Pastor Finley was born and raised in Baltimore, Maryland. He graduated from Mount Saint Mary's University with a BA degree in Sociology with a Criminal Justice Concentration. While there, he was named to the Who's Who List, of American Colleges and Universities and received his commission and served as a Lieutenant in the United States Army.

Pastor Finley is the husband of Lady Tiffanie Finley; father of four sons: Paul II, Cameron, Zion and Allan; two daughters: Brieonia and Kai as well as one granddaughter, Nu'or. He treasures the great call and responsibility God has entrusted to his leadership. With a keen awareness of eternal values, Pastor Finley stays cognizant of his calling and remains uncompromisingly faithful to the preaching of the gospel, the foundational principles of holiness and the promotion of the Kingdom agenda.

Connect: Website: www.lionofjudahworshipcenter.org
            Email: ljwc761@gmail.com
            FB: @LJWC761
            IG: @LJWC761
            YouTube: LJWC761 Lion of Judah Worship

Terralyn Frazier

Terralyn Frazier is an American author, editor, and former English teacher. She is a mother, wife, daughter, and sister.

Growing up in a Christian home, Terralyn is no stranger to prayer and its necessity. Understanding that prayer is the connector between God's desire and man's execution of it, she knows that living life without prayer is certain failure. Terralyn's conviction about prayer and confidence in Christ led her to co-author a prayer book/workbook with her sister.

As a teen, Terralyn was often asked to pray for friends and teammates. Her passion and understanding of prayer grew organically throughout the years until the W.O.R.D. Ministry, a non-profit organization, was birthed. Terralyn is currently expanding her entrepreneurial exploits in the field of copy editing as a freelance editor.

Terralyn can often be found preparing lessons and scheduling guests for her weekly Facebook and newly created YouTube social media ministry platforms: Women of Restoration and Deliverance (W.O.R.D.). These ministry platforms were created to empower women to live their ministry call out loud--confidently and unapologetically.

Contact: Terralynfrazier@msn.com
Facebook: Terralyn Simon-Frazier, Women of Restoration and Deliverance
YouTube: Women of Restoration and Deliverance

Toni G. Guy

Toni G. Guy is a native of Baltimore, Maryland. She accepted Christ as her savior at age 11 and has spent her life demonstrating God's love through service to others. She believes prayer is our lifeline to God and it deepens our connection with God.

Toni currently is a member of Walk by Faith Ministries in Baltimore, Maryland, under the leadership of Reverend Damon Dorsey. She is passionate about spreading the gospel, praying with and for others, Christian education, and serving others. Toni serves on the Intercessory and Prayer Ministry, the Grief Recovery Ministry, HMA2 (the Outreach Ministry), and the Children's Ministry at Walk by Faith Ministries.

Toni is a graduate of Lincoln University and is currently employed in the Biotech Industry. She is a consultant for Paparazzi Accessories, a licensed insurance agent. She is also the owner of Building Our Legacies Together, LLC, a consulting firm dedicated to helping others accomplish their dreams. Toni currently resides in Baltimore, MD, and is the mother of two children, Tyler and Adrienne.

One of Toni's favorite scriptures is Philippians 4:6 *Do not worry about anything, but in everything by prayer and supplication with thanksgiving let your requests be made known to God. And the peace of God, which surpasses all understanding, will guard your hearts and your minds in Christ Jesus.*

Contact: Facebook : Toni Guy
           Email : tonigguy@qmail.com

Evangelist Elaine Harmon

I was born in Baltimore, MD., to Richard and Alberta Hall, who lived in a small, low-income, all Black neighborhood named Cherry Hill. Although poor, we five children thought of ourselves as richly blessed because our parents worked hard to provide for us. We were raised in a house full of love by a stern, but fair father who was grounded in the Lord Jesus Christ and a loving saved mother who frequently had to intercede for us with our father as well as with God. Even when Momma was *not* attending church, she would still awaken her five children every Sunday morning to prepare us to attend Sunday School. We attended church dressed in our "Sunday best." Attending Sunday School and Morning worship was a requirement, not an option. In our youth, it pleased us not to have to go at any other time.

After graduating from Coppin State College, I married my now longtime partner, Stanley Harmon, who relocated us to Philadelphia, PA. We both received a Master's degree from Temple University. We also have raised three children in Philadelphia. Although my life did not always reflect Christ, I have always believed in God. I grew up not just appreciating church, but I always had a deep appreciation for God. Thankfully, He saved me in 1985 while attending Christ Mission of the Apostolic Faith. I became an ordained minister in 2010. Since 1985 I have been a Bible teacher and involved with various Outreach Ministries. As with other brothers and sisters in Christ, soul-winning is my goal. It is a privilege to participate in the *If My People Book Project*. I'm praying that this book will help the reader move closer to God.

Contact: ev77harm@gmail.com

Minister Melissa Powell-Harrell

Melissa Harrell is an ordained minister and a devout woman of faith. Having acquired the majority of her education in Baltimore City Public School system, Harrell is a proud alumna of Annapolis High school. Consequently, she earned an undergraduate degree in 2002 from Morgan State University. Then in 2004, she acquired Master's Degree in Social Work from Widener University.

Married to Mr. Marvin Harrell, and the mother of two "anointed and beautiful" children: Adah and Malachi.

March 31, 2005, she accepted her call as a preacher of the gospel. Consequently, she earned a Master of Divinity in May 2015 from United Theological Seminary. She is the owner and director of *Transforming Lives Counseling Services* (TLCS).

In 2021, Harrell made her authorship debut with the release of *Poems From The Heart*, then weeks later, after becoming one of 62 co-authors to collectively assemble *Soulful Affirmations: 365 Days Of Positive Thoughts And Lessons to Start Your Day*.

Prayer is important to me because I have seen God's power in my life. I am a recipient of God's miracles, signs, and wonders

    Contact :   mpowell7611@yahoo.com
                      https://www.phenomenalwomanmin.com

Minister Mishawn A. Jones

Mishawn is a retired educator from Howard County Public School System. She was born and raised in Baltimore, MD, and is a graduate of Baltimore Polytechnic Institute. She received her Bachelor of Science in Elementary Education with a Minor in Mathematics from Morgan State University. She has two Master's degrees in School Guidance Counseling and School Administration and Supervision from Loyola College in Maryland and Johns Hopkins University.

In 2011, Mishawn was licensed as a Minister under the leadership of Rev. Dr. Stephen J. Russell, Jr., at Calvary Baltimore (formerly Calvary Baptist Church). During her tenure at Calvary, she served as the Minister of New Life & Care Ministry. Currently, Mishawn serves as a Minister at Walk By Faith Ministries, where Rev. Damon Dorsey is Pastor. She aspires to continue her pursuit in religious studies and would like to work in church administration.

Mishawn is the proud mother of two adult daughters, Chelsea and Kailyn and the very proud grandmother of Olivia, Ava and Anderson, who affectionately call her "Cookie." Mishawn enjoys spending time with her parents and family; bowling, traveling, cooking, and listening to music. If you ever need a good laugh or a dose of reality, she's your girl!

Contact:: Majenterprises48@gmail.com
FB - Mishawn Jones
IG - Shawnie108

Cynthia Knight

Cynthia Knight is a writer, blogger, and author of three books: the fiction novel *Whyte Chocolate* and two editions of *Big Mama Wisdom for Couples: 205 Questions to Ask and Discuss before Marriage*. Cynthia knows first-hand the power of prayer. She was led by the Holy Spirit to coordinate and compile the *If My People* book project. She hopes the life-changing impact of prayer will manifest in the lives of others through this work.

Cynthia is the spiritual sister to the Lion of Judah Worship Center, where she served as Church Administrator for many years before transitioning to Kingdom Life Church in Baltimore, Maryland, under the leadership of Pastor Michael and Anita Phillips. Since the onset of the pandemic, she now worships virtually with Pastor Michael and Anita Phillips as an e-Member at the Potters House in Dallas, Texas.

A self-proclaimed "lover of words," Cynthia's early years usually found her captivated by fiction books, romantic comedies, and musicals. Her respect and admiration for these art forms piqued her interest in writing. Eventually, Cynthia's love for writing led her to attend the University of Maryland College Park as an English Major. She graduated with a Bachelor of Arts degree in Arts & Humanities. Cynthia is a Chief Human Resources Officer and HR Consultant in her professional life, and she holds a Master of Science degree in Management and Human Resources.

Cynthia is the owner and CEO of Mosaic Consortium Group, LLC., the parent company to Onyx Gavel Publishing, from which she publishes her titles. Cynthia resides in Baltimore County, Maryland, and enjoys crocheting, entertaining, and spending time with her husband of 29 years and two adult children.

You can follow Cynthia and her blog, The Complex Collective, at www.CynthiaLKnight.com or www.ComplexCollective.com.

Minister Michelle Lee

Minister Michelle Lee is an Associate Minister at Walk By Faith Ministries, under the leadership of Rev. Damon Dorsey. She accepted her call to Ministry in January 2018. Currently, she's the Servant Leader of the Grief Recovery Ministry and also serves on the Outreach Ministry, Intercessory and Prayer Ministry, and teaches Bible Study.

While she works full time as a Victim & Witness Advocacy Coordinator for the Office of the State's Attorney for Baltimore City, she also serves as a Chaplain and District Coordinator with the Baltimore Police Department Chaplaincy Program. As a proud Veteran of the United States Army, she's a dedicated member of the Paul Thompson DAV Chapter, where she is the former chapter Chaplain and currently serving as the 2nd Junior Vice-Commander. In 2019, she was named Veteran of The Year. Much like Dorcas, she loves serving God's people with comfort, compassion, and empathy. When time permits, Minister Michelle volunteers at Roberta's House Family Grief Support Center, supporting teenagers navigating the grief process.

Currently, Minister Michelle is pursuing her Bachelor's Degree in Christian Counseling from West Coast Bible College and Seminary, graduating in 2022, and plans to pursue her Master's Degree and Life Coaching Certification.

Minister Michelle is the loving wife of her biggest supporter, her husband Curtis Lee, and they believe that all things are possible with God and Prayer. Pray, Live, Love and Laugh is their motto. Minister Michelle is the sole proprietor of Pure Gold Inspirations, LLC

Contact: FB: Chelle Nothavnit Lee
IG: Puregoldinspirations
Email: PureGoldInspirations@gmail.com

HOLLY MAGNUSON

Holly Magnuson is a global HR and talent leader with leadership and consulting experiences in various global Fortune 500 companies and non-profit organizations, including GE, Hershey, TE Connectivity, and Chewy. Her passion is to equip leaders and build up the next generation.

Holly received her Masters of Industrial and Labor Relations from Cornell University and B.S. in Pre-Professional Psychology at Geneva College. Originally from "almost Heaven," West Virginia, she now lives in South Florida with her family and two crazy dogs. She is honored to be a part of Christ Fellowship Church in Palm Beach Gardens, where her husband, Josh, serves as a pastor, and she serves on the CF Worship Team.

Renee Myers

Hailing from East Baltimore, MD, Renee Myers is a resilient soul. Faced with childhood obstacles and feelings of not being good enough, she persisted to surpass her circumstances. Her friends became family and brought her to know Christ. Since then, she has used her past hurt and love of God to help transform the lives of others.

In the Lord's pursuit of Renee, he decided to use her best friend at that time to introduce her to the saving power of Jesus Christ. Renee has a tremendous love for young people who are often misunderstood. Remarkably, the Lord has used many aspects of her testimony especially from her youth to help others allowing her to attest to the fact that "All things work together for the good to them who love God and are called according to his purpose (Romans 8:28)."

Renee is also a dedicated mother of three children: Shantae', Tavon Jr, and Jessica. She also serves her community in various outreach efforts in Baltimore. She is the founder and Prayer warrior of the Facebook Prayer group called "When We Pray." She is striving daily to continue her healing and growth in order to be the best version of herself.

Contact: To connect with Renee, you can follow her on social media as @ReneeMyers and @blessedhandsbyRenee.
Also please feel free to visit her first books on Instagram @avoychbookpage.

Nicki Nichols

Nicki Nichols is a visionary, Kingdom builder, teacher, and entrepreneur. Through her obedience, God led her to launch, Seeking God for 14 Days...The Prayer Experience—a transformative, purpose-driven walk with God. For weeks, she graciously opened her heart, sharing the word of God during nightly prayer sessions. This calling expanded when God spoke to her and announced that her assignment was not yet done. She was then instructed to continue her journey, "Up. Onward. Forward. March." And so she did. Along with dozens of prayer warriors, psalmists, and preachers, Nicki hosted "14 Hour of Prayer Live," a Facebook Live event seen by more than 14,000 people worldwide.

A true believer and follower of the Word of God, Nicki had no technical experience to guide her through what God had assigned, but her obedience shepherded her along this path. She describes her relations with God as 'simple.' "He talks, I listen. I pray, He answers, and I follow His instructions no matter how far-fetched it may seem. Even if I personally feel unqualified for the task."

Nicki continues to fulfill God's purpose to usher God's children into His presence so that God's plan for the "Kingdom Remnant" can be revealed. From this revelation, Vision Conference was born. Vision Conference is a two-day God-inspired event where the spirit of God is given free rein to provide clarity and teach us how to live the life He predestined us to, with all power and authority, to the obedience of Christ.

Contact:: Instagram @NickiNichols18

Elder Elect Sonja Owens

Sonja Owens is currently an Elect Elder of Kingdom Lovers International Ministries, under the pastoral leadership of Overseer Lewis Lambert Sr. At an early age, she was exposed to and taught of many powerful and miraculous works of the Spirit and God began to reveal the gifts of the Spirit to her and continued to show her the miraculous into her teenage years. At the age of 25, God began to open His Word to her and gave her a burning desire for prayer, souls, evangelism, and ministry. As many of us do, she ran from the call of God and even tried to hide. Unable to run any longer and weighted by the glory of God and His powerful anointing on her life, she said, "yes, Lord."

As God has permitted, she often preaches, teaches Bible study, has been doing prison ministry since 2006, feeds the Homeless and evangelizes in the streets of Baltimore snatching treasures out of darkness to the glory of God. God has opened doors for her to travel to various locations sharing her testimony, leading souls to Christ, and preaching/ teaching the gospel.

God has allowed her to spend 5 months in the Bronx, hitting the streets, leading souls to Christ and helping many Women in areas like Hunts Point get out of addiction, prostitution, off the streets and into treatment. She spent 2 months in California hitting the streets at LA's Skid Row and to the glory of God has spent a week in Amsterdam evangelizing in the Red-Light District. God has allowed her to also preach at several services/ conferences in the Bronx, Delaware and West Virginia.

Elder Elect Sonja is on a mission to bring souls to Christ and assist others in getting free of the powers of darkness through healing and deliverance. It is her heart's desire to take the gospel into all the earth, setting the captives free and making disciples under the unction and power of the Holy Spirit.

"I thank God for every trial, fiery furnace and storm that He has allowed me to crawl, run, roll and soar through. For they have truly been the training

ground for the oil and powerful anointing He has allowed me to possess."

"But as it is written:
Eye has not seen, nor ear heard,
Nor have entered into the heart of man
The things which God has prepared for those who love Him."
1 Car. 2:9

Contact: Email: sowens8@outlook.com
               Facebook: Sonja Owens
               IG: eaglewings8

Brian Pinson

Brian Pinson, a native son of Baltimore, Maryland, attends Walk By Faith Ministries located in Baltimore, Maryland, under the spiritual leadership of Reverend Damon A. Dorsey. He is active in several ministries at Walk By Faith Ministries. Brian is a member of the WBF Media Team, the WBF Intercessory and Prayer, the WBF Grief Recovery Ministries. He also has led and conducted Bible Studies throughout the year at Walk By Faith Ministries.

He is currently pursuing his Associates of Arts degree at Baltimore City Community College in general studies, and his plans is to transfer to a four-year college or university.

One of his passions is photography, and the other is traveling. Brian has his own photography business Blackinkpin Photography and has had his photography published and displayed in several online exhibitions.

Brian has five children Kori Pinson (deceased), Tavion Robinson, Patrick Robinson Jr., Kristopher Stanley, and Tamara Pinson.

The reason I think prayer is important is because God wants us to have a relationship with our Heavenly Father every day. When we pray to God, we allow God to know what is going on with us in our lives. We also build a line of communication with God, it builds a stronger relationship with God, and our trust and faith grow with the intimate time with God.

Psalms 5:1-3 (NLT) reads as follows: *O Lord, hear me as I pray; pay attention to my groaning. Listen to my cry for help, my King and my God, for I pray to no one but you. Listen to my voice each morning, LORD. Each morning I bring my requests to you and wait expectantly.*

Contact: You can follow Brian Pinson on social media, Facebook and Instagram @Brian Pinson.

Elder Alicia A. Richardson

In 1995, Alicia A. Richardson accepted Christ as her Lord and Savior and received the baptism of the Holy Spirit while attending the Church of the Redeemed of the Lord (CRL). The Lord began speaking to her in the year 2000 regarding the call to ministry. On March 31, 2002, He simply said, "I AM calling you." She acknowledged His call in 2003 and accepted in 2005, completing the CRL Ministerial Training Program in 2006. Continuing in the faith and service of Jesus Christ, Alicia later accepted her appointment to eldership in 2012 and was formally ordained in 2014.

An avid volunteer, Elder Richardson is passionate about building the Kingdom and has served in various support and leadership capacities over the years. One of her life scriptures is *Colossians 3:23-24*, *"Whatsoever ye do, do it heartily, as to the Lord, and not unto men. Knowing that of the Lord ye shall receive the reward of inheritance: for ye serve the Lord Christ."* She also has a passion for seeing people walk in true freedom, liberated by the Gospel of Jesus Christ, in fellowship with one another" *(I John 6)*, as demonstrated by her volunteer service where she is walking out *Micah 6:8*. Elder Richardson currently serves at the Araminta Freedom Initiative, which aims to bring healing, restoration, justice, and true freedom to survivors of sex trafficking. Most recently, she has taken an interest in Live Baltimore, a nonprofit which works to grow Baltimore's economy by attracting residents, supporting healthy housing markets, and retaining residents of Baltimore City.

Elder Richardson holds a master's degree from Loyola University in spiritual and pastoral care (faith and social justice) and a bachelor's in English from the University of Baltimore, where she is currently pursuing a certificate in Trauma-Informed Care. She has been married to her loving husband and best friend, Keith, Sr., for thirty-seven years. Together they have four children: Shekia, Darrell, Keith, J. and Kevin, who have blessed them with a quiver of grands and great-grandchildren alike.

Contact: Psalm63AR@gmail.com

Amanda B. Sumiel

As an undergrad majoring in English at the University of Maryland College Park, Amanda's dream was to write cards for Hallmark. For many, this may sound peculiar, but for Amanda, it was in line with her love for writing. She wrote poetry throughout her years at UMCP as a stress reliever and in her spare time. After graduation, joining the workforce, marriage, and two kids, there has been very little time to write, but it is still one of her passions. She is happily married to her husband, Winston, for 22 years, and their union has produced two incredible young men, Jordan and Justin. Amanda is an HR Professional, MixxedFit Instructor, and Pampered Chef Consultant, but her most important title is Jesus Girl. She is not ashamed to proclaim her love and devotion to the Lord. She says, "It is only because of Him that I am." She is an active member in her church, The House of Prayer Gospel Assembly, and strongly believes that prayer is an essential part of her Christian journey. "Prayer," she says, "is her daily talk with God". "In prayer, I can release my innermost thoughts, relay my honor and gratefulness, and refresh my connection with the Father."

Contact: Facebook: Amanda Burrell Sumiel
            Instagram: Sugarandspice0708
            Email: absumiel69@gmail.com

Bridgette L. Threat

Bridgette L. Threat, a native of Brooklyn, New York, is a minister of the gospel and an accomplished Social Work professional and advocate. Bridgette has always possessed a heart to help others and encourage them to live life to its fullest potential. This desire to help and encourage others led Bridgette to pursue and obtain Master's degrees in Social Work and Christian Ministries. It also leads her to share her passion for prayer. She believes that prayer is an essential part of life because it reveals the heart and mind of God. Bridgette shares that prayer helps us become one with the Father and have a real relationship with Him. And in doing so, it helps people to live to their fullest potential.

Bridgette loves talking and helping people. She is the founder of Starting Point Therapeutic Counseling, LLC, where they passionately strive to see those who are suffering from loss of any kinds find hope and strength to start over again. Bridgette feels privileged to work with her clients and to be allowed into an emotionally vulnerable space with the simple goal of helping.

Bridgette proudly served in the United States Air Force Reserve and Army for 32 years before retiring in August 2020. She is the proud wife-of Felix Threat, mother of four adult children, Demetrius, Megan, Shayla, and Morgan and four grandchildren, Taylor, Kai, Tyler and Eli, has worked diligently to instill values of hard work and service to humanity in the lives of her children, family members, and friends.

Contact: blthreat@startingpointherapeuticcounseling.com

Minister Dunia Kambon-Thornton

Minister Dunia has devoted her life to God in true worship and desires to be used to motivate, inspire, and arouse the Body of Christ to worship God in Spirit and in Truth. At the tender age of 19, she accepted her call and preached her initial sermon at New Antioch Church (NAC). She served at NAC, under the leadership Bishop Orlando Wilson, as an Associate Minster for 17 years. She is now serving as an Associate Minister at Greater Paradise Christian Center under the leadership of Bishop Shawn Bell. Minister Thornton has over 22 years of ministry experience and is guided mainly by *Proverbs 3:5-6 "Trust in the Lord will all your heart; do not depend on your own understanding. Seek his will in all you do, and he will show you which path to take."* Minister Dunia Thornton believes that prayer is the gateway for intimacy with God.

Contact: Facebook: Dunia Kambon-Thornton
           Instagram: @kambonthornton

Terry Wedlock

I am a mother of 3 young men, a hairstylist and a student in God's class of renewal. The season of Covid -19 was my wake-up call. I lost a lot, learned a lot and have been forever changed. God decided that it was my reason to be dug up, pruned, and replanted in his word, leadership, trust, and mercy. God has been gracefully ushering me out of my comfort zone. My time of pausing from fear, jumping in too fast from impatience and missing opportunities from being disobedient have come to an end. I hope you enjoy my testimonies of honesty, openness and rawness. I wrote about my conversations with my father during one of the most challenging yet eye-opening seasons in my life. Change can be scary. Trusting can be uncomfortable. Allowing God to direct your path will always be mind-blowing!

Contact: Instagram @TerryWedlock

Dr. Toyia K. Younger

Dr. Toyia K. Younger assumed the position of Senior Vice President for Student Affairs at Iowa State University on August 17, 2020. In this role, she provides strategic leadership to the division, which encompasses a broad and diverse portfolio of departments, offices, and teams organized into three units: the Dean of Students Office, Student Health and Wellness, and Campus Life, each led by an Associate Vice President. Her 20-year career in higher education includes work on a variety of colleges and universities across the nation, in one of the largest higher education systems in the country, and at two national associations.

Dr. Younger considers herself a marketplace minister. She has both a national and international reach and an amazing network, both personally and professional, which has created numerous opportunities for her to share her story and encourage others. Her mission is to ignite a passion for God in others by helping women learn how to embrace their true selves and live an authentic life. Dr. Younger believes her life's story is a manifestation of Proverbs 18:26; your gift will make room for you and bring you before great men. She has been invited to speak all over the country at national meetings, youth and women's day services and has served as a motivational speaker to women and young adults for over a decade. The heartbeat of her ministry is characterized by her prayer life and her desire to be a living expression of God's grace. Dr. Younger considers herself a "daughter of grace" whom God is using to speak words of hope, inspiration, and direction to His people. She is a woman who teaches practically, operates empathetically, and ministers prophetically.

Dr. Younger is one of the spiritual daughters of Pastors Timothy and Tanya Stokes of Family Worship Center Church International, located in Flint, Michigan. Under their leadership, God allowed her to serve almost a decade in various capacities in ministry. She currently serves with Dr. Jazz Ministries and attends Victory Grace Center in Bladensburg, Maryland. A native of Flint, Michigan, she holds a doctorate in Education Policy from the University of Maryland College Park, a Master of Arts in Counseling from Trinity University and a Bachelor of Arts in Social Relations from Michigan State University. Dr. Younger is the daughter of the late Bishop Odis A. Floyd, 2nd presiding Bishop Emeritus and one of the Founders of the Full Gospel Baptist Church Fellowship under the leadership of Bishop Paul S. Morton.

    Contact: FB: Toyia K. Younger
                     Twitter: toyia_younger

REFERENCES

"Access Your Bible from Anywhere." *BibleGateway.com: A Searchable Online Bible in over 150 Versions and 50 Languages.*, https://www.biblegateway.com/.

Barbour Publishing Inc. (2011). Holy Bible: King James Version Burgundy genuine bonded leather study Bible. Barbour Pub. Genesis 1. (n.d.). https://my.bible.com/bible

Bible gateway passage: 2 Corinthians 10:5 - American standard version. (n.d.). Bible Gateway. https://www.biblegateway.com/passage/?search=2+Corinthians+10%3A5&version=ASV

Bible gateway passage: Ecclesiastes 9:11 - King James Version. (n.d.). Bible Gateway. https://www.biblegateway.com/passage/?search=Ecclesiastes+9%3A11&version=KJV

Bible gateway passage: Matthew 16:26 - New King James Version. (n.d.). Bible Gateway. https://www.biblegateway.com/passage/?search=Matthew+16%3A26&version=NKJV

C.I. Scofield, D.D. (2013). The Scofield Study Bible-KJV. Oxford, NY. Oxford University Press.

Drake Publishing King James Version Lawrenceville Georgia 30046 Copyright 1999 Ninth Printing October 2011

Harmon, J. (2020). Letter to God. From *Letter to God Stage Play*. JPE Music BMI.

Holy Bible: New King James Version Personal Size Reference Bible, Brown, Leather touch. Holman Bible Staff. (2013). Holman Bible Pub.

King James Bible. (2017). King James Bible Online. https://www.kingjamesbibleonline.org/ (Original work published 1769)

Meyer, J. (2018). The Everyday Life Bible. New York: Hachette Book Group.

Meyer, J. (2021). In Search of Wisdom. New York: Hachette Book Group.

Nelson, T. (2005). *KJV, reference Bible, eBook: Holy Bible, King James Version*. Thomas Nelson. (n.d.). OFFICIAL KING JAMES BIBLE ONLINE. https://www.kingjamesbibleonline.org/

Nelson, T. (2005). *NKJV, holy Bible, eBook: Holy Bible, new King James Version*. Thomas Nelson.

Nelson, T. (2020). *NKJV scripture journal - Genesis: Holy Bible, new King*

James Version. Thomas Nelson.

New International Version (2021). NIV Online. The https://youversion.com/the-bible-app/ Bible App - YouVersion

Scofield, C. I., & Rikkers, D. W. (Eds.). (2003). KJV Scofield Study Bible (2003 ed.). Oxford University Press, Inc.

Scofield, C., & Rikkers, D. W. (2003), Philippians 3:14. In SCOFIELD study Bible , KJV . essay, Oxford University Press.

Sri, E. P., & Teresa, M. (2017). Chapter 5- Sharing in the Sword. In Walking with Mary: A biblical journey from Nazareth to the Cross (pp. 101–102). essay, Image.

The Holy Bible, King James Version, Harper Collins Christian Publishing 2021. Online

Tyndale, & Tyndale House Publishers. (2004). *Life application study Bible: New living translation*. Tyndale House Publishers.

Tyndale. *NLT life application study Bible (Hardcover)*. 3rd ed., 2019.

Tyndale House Publishers. (2017). *NLT study Bible: New living translation*. Psalms 139:1

Tyndale House Publishers. (2017). *NLT study Bible: New living translation*. Psalms 30:5

Tyndale House Publishers. (2017). *NLT study Bible: New living translation*. Hebrews 11:1

Tyndale House. *NLT Praise and Worship Study Bible (Softcover).*, 1997.

www.ingramcontent.com/pod-product-compliance
Lightning Source LLC
Chambersburg PA
CBHW051947290426
44110CB00015B/2145